ESSENTIAL SELECTIVE THINKING SKILLS

5 Thinking Skills Test Papers

RAY LEE | JIMMY LIU

To Cookie, my light,
and to Phoebe who I hope
can one day figure out all the questions in this book.

Five Senses Education Pty Ltd
2/195 Prospect Highway
Seven Hills 2147
New South Wales Australia

First Published 2023

Lee, Ray and Liu, Jimmy

Essential Selective
Thinking Skills Book 2
ISBN 978-1-76032-544-2

2023 02 17

Contents

Preface

This book is designed to help students prepare for the Selective High School Placement Test. It consists of five thinking skills practice exam papers and is suitable for use by Year 5 and 6 students. The exam papers are designed to the exact format of the Selective High School Placement Test, with hand picked questions that closely relate to past Selective High School Examination questions.

Success in this extremely competitive exam requires commitment and hard work. We hope these practice exam papers can help you achieve your goals.

Five Senses Education

Selective Practice Test Paper
Thinking Skills 6 (Time allowed: 40 min)

INSTRUCTIONS

1. Write your Name on the cover page.
2. There are 40 questions in this paper. For each question there are four possible answers, A, B, C and D. Choose the one correct answer and record your choice on the separate answer sheet. If you make a mistake, erase thoroughly and try again.
3. You will not lose marks for incorrect answers, so you should attempt all 40 questions
4. You must complete the answer sheet within the time limit. There will not be any extra time at the end of the exam to record your answers on the answer sheet.
5. You can use the question paper for working out, but no extra paper is allowed.

Name: ______________________________

1 Consider these three shapes

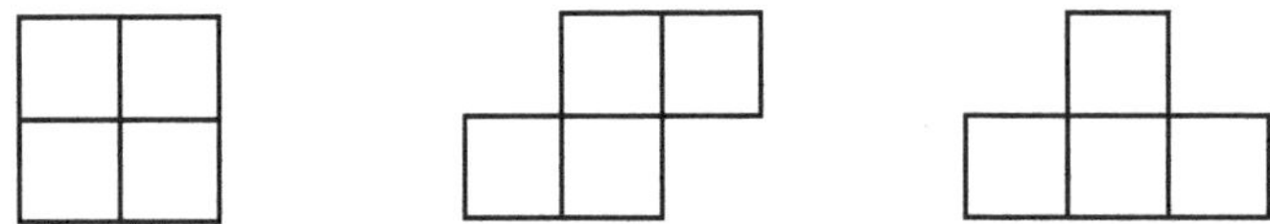

Which of the following cannot be made using each shape once only, without flipping, cutting or overlapping?

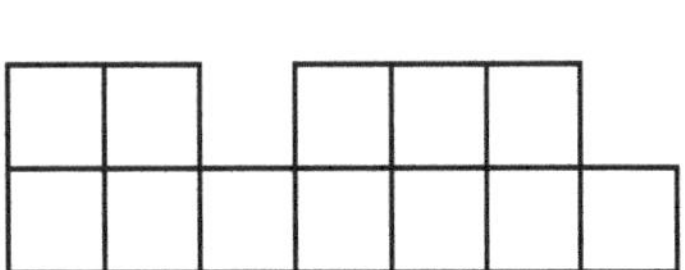

A

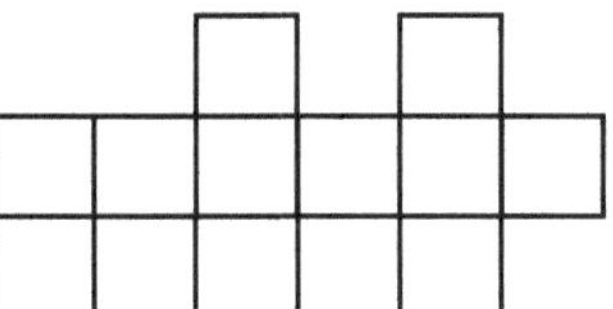

B

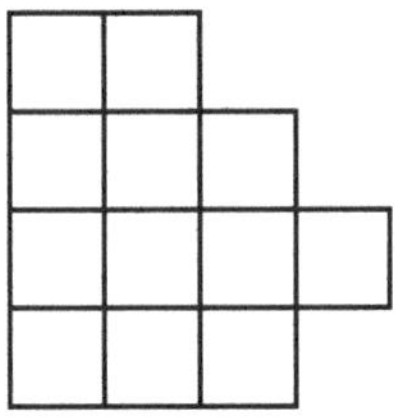

C

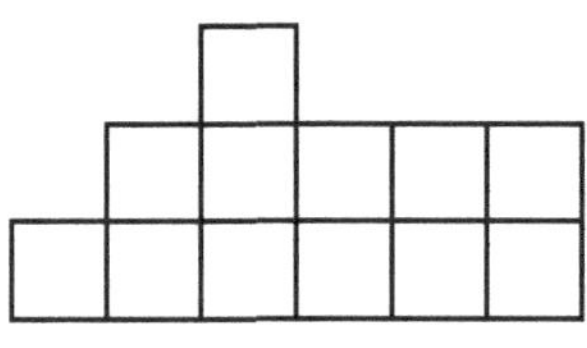

D

2 Communication is the backbone of our society. It allows us to form connections, influence decisions, and motivate change. Public speaking is one of the most important and dreaded forms of communication.

Which of the following, if true, most **strengthens** the argument above?

A Communication is not vital to society, rather it is a specialised skill.
B Having these skills is beneficial in the long run especially when one works.
C Public speaking helps people to overcome their fears.
D Communication allows individuals to develop greater fears in the future.

3 Kent Police have put out a tender for heating maintenance and installation. Below are quotes from 3 suppliers.

Heating maintenance and installation	Supplier 1 Total cost over 3 years ($)	Supplier 2 Total cost over 2 years ($)	Supplier 3 Total cost over 5 years ($)
Installation and boiler replacements	24,000	18,000	36,000
Hot Air Systems	15,000	10,000	25,000
Service and maintenance	17,000	12,000	25,000

Amongst all three suppliers, based on an annual cost, what is the average cost to install hot air systems?

A $5000
B $6000
C $7000
D $8000

4 An advertisement for hair dye claims:

MULTI has the fastest setting hair dye as it only takes 30 minutes!

This claim was tested by using four different hair dyes, and two questions asked:

Hair Dye	*Was it a MULTI hair dye?*	*Was the hair dyed in 30 minutes?*
1	Yes	**(a)**
2	**(b)**	Yes
3	**(c)**	No
4	No	**(d)**

Which **two** answers **must** be known to test the claim that the advertisement makes?

A **a** and **b**.
B **a** and **c**.
C **c** and **d**.
D **b** and **c**.

5 If Nelly writes notes after class, she is better prepared for her spontaneous class tests.

If she doesn't do well in these class tests then she will be less prepared for the end of term exam.

If she does well in her end of term exam, she will have a score above 80%.

If the above statements are correct, which of the following is possible?

A Nelly not writing notes after class will mean she will not score above 80% on the end of term test.
B Nelly doing well in her class test will lead to a score below 80% on the end of term test.
C Nelly being less prepared for the class test means she wrote her notes after class.
D Nelly doing well in her exam means she didn't do well in the class test.

6 In a survey of juice lovers, everyone who liked apple did not like cranberry, but everyone who liked cranberry liked guava. Everyone who liked orange liked apple.

Luke, John, Dan and Han all took part in the survey.

Based on the information above, which of the following is **not** true?

A If Luke likes apple juice, he doesn't like guava juice.
B If John doesn't like cranberry juice, he likes orange juice.
C If Dan doesn't like apple juice, he likes orange juice.
D If Han likes orange juice, he doesn't like cranberry juice.

7 A song playlist plays random songs if there are less than seven songs in it.

Diana: "Wow is this a new song you added to the playlist? I've never heard it before."

Cam: "No I didn't add this, so you must added it.

If the information in the box is true, whose reasoning is correct?

- **A** Diana only.
- **B** Cam only.
- **C** Both Diana and Cam.
- **D** Neither Diana nor Cam.

8 Choose a figure which would most closely resemble the unfolded form of given figure.

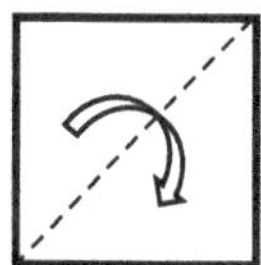
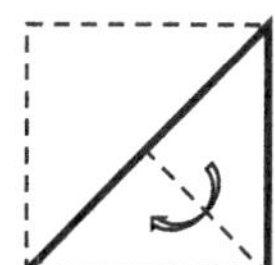
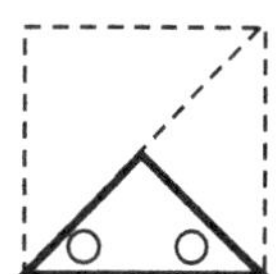

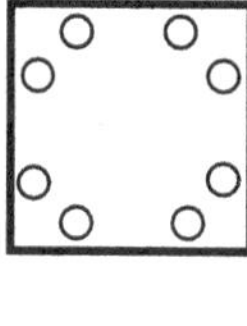

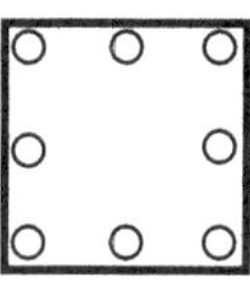
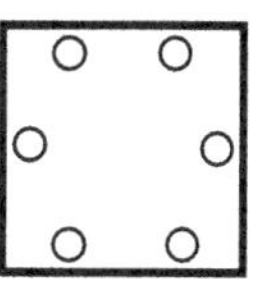
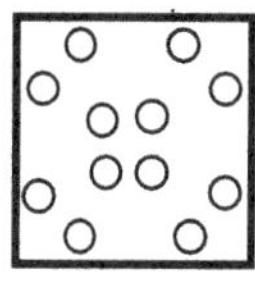

A **B** **C** **D**

9 Ink jet printers are often very cheap. That is because they're sold at cost, or even at a loss — the manufacturer either makes no profit from the printer itself or loses money. These are very affordable and tend to come with complimentary ink.

Which of the following, if true, most **weakens** the argument above?

- **A** Printers may be cheap but printer ink is more expensive than the actual printer.
- **B** The more expensive the printer is, the fancier it is.
- **C** Printers have always been a useful household item to have.
- **D** It is cheaper to produce printers than its ink.

10 Minghao enters a national art competition that has the purpose to find new, aspiring painters. Each year the competition provides a certain theme that artists must incorporate into their work. They are interested in unseen and unusual styles and mediums of art. Awards will be given to first, second and third place, as well as a people's choice award.

All painters must have the work in by a certain date to be considered for the competition. Minghao created an unusual art piece that has many people talking, however he handed it in a day late of the due date.

Despite Minghao handing in his piece a day late and not having his name on the official voting sheet, why did he receive the people's choice award?

A The judges really liked his work they allowed him to be considered.
B An overwhelming number of people wrote his name down on the ballots despite it not being there.
C His work was so unusual that people were not impressed.
D The deadline was a lie, they accepted anyone to be considered for the competition.

11 Five people are standing next to each other in a line, with the first person near the flowerpot to the last person at the door. They all have different ages and favourite colours. We know that:

- The 23-year-old person in the middle likes green and is two people away from the person who is 22.
- The 19-year-old has three people to their right, with the 3rd a 25-year-old person.
- The person who likes red is four people away from the person who likes purple.
- The 22-year-old is next to the person who likes yellow.
- The 19-year-old person likes yellow.

Using the information above, in what position is the oldest person?

A First.
B Second.
C Fourth.
D Fifth.

12 A survey was carried out of 100 people in each of the 4 towns to determine their voting intentions at the next election. The results are shown below:

	Labor Party	Liberal Party	Greens Party	One nation Party
Ashfield	30	30	20	20
Baulkham Hills	40	30	20	10
Castle Hill	50	20	20	10
Denistone	25	25	25	25

The local newspaper is presenting 4 pie charts to illustrate the results. The graphic artist has just drawn the outline of the first graph, but cannot remember which town it represents. The parties are not necessarily in the same order on the pie chart as they are in the table.

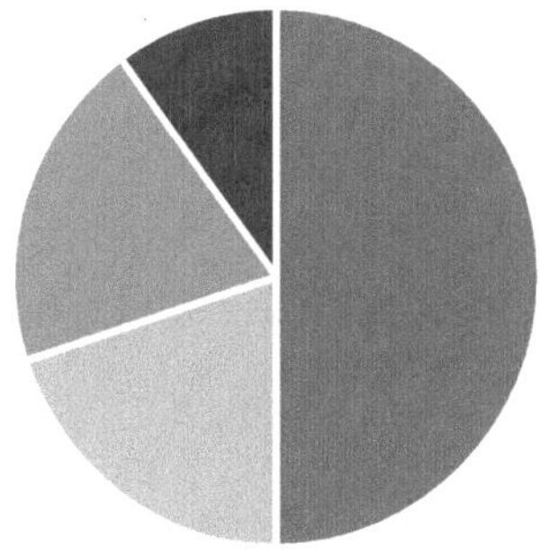

Which town does the pie chart represent?

A Ashfield
B Baulkham Hills
C Castle Hill
D Denistone

13 Woo is hiding behind a door. Each door has two statements, some true, some false. However, no more than one statement is false on each box.

Door 1	*Door 2*	*Door 3*
I am not behind door 1.	My name is Woo.	My name is Zi.
I am behind door 2.	I am not behind door 2	I am behind door 3.

Based on the information above, which of the following must be true?

A My name is Zi.
B I am behind door 1.
C I am behind door 3.
D I am behind door 2.

14 Maddie has created a program that allows a person to play tic-tac-toe against the computer which never loses, using the traditional X's and O's.

Naomi: "I'm playing your program right now and I think I'm going to win since there is a W on the board."

Maddie: "That's not right, you aren't going to win since that isn't supposed to happen!"

If the information in the box is true, whose reasoning is correct?

A Naomi only.
B Maddie only.
C Both Naomi and Maddie.
D Neither Naomi nor Maddie.

15 Nicole's class appoints a class monitor per week. There are 23 people in her class and Nicole has had a turn in the first term.

Nicole: "Since I already had a turn, I won't have one for the rest of the year!"

Which of the following sentences reveals Nicole's mistake?

A She forgot about the new kids who can join their class throughout the year.
B All the boys in her class are given the role of class monitor twice.
C Her classmates vote for the person they want to be the class monitor.
D She has the chance to be class monitor again since there are 40 school weeks in the school year.

16 Between which two points is the train traveling at the slowest rate?

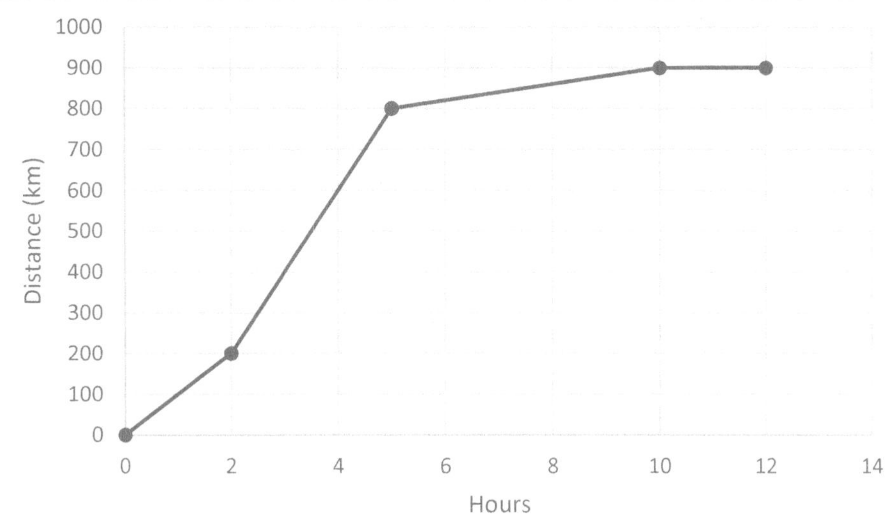

A between 0 and 2 hours
B between 2 and 5 hours
C between 5 and 10 hours
D between 10 and 12 hours

17 Joon wanted to figure out what is the most popular fruit at school: banana, apple, grape and orange. They did a survey of all the students at the school, and found the following:

- No one enjoyed both grapes and oranges.
- All who enjoyed bananas enjoyed grapes.
- People who don't dislike oranges enjoy apples.
- There are more people who enjoy bananas than apples.

Which was the most popular fruit?

A Apple.
B Grape.
C Banana.
D Orange.

18 It wasn't long ago that coding was seen by many as an odd hobby for geeks tinkering with computers in their basements. But over the past several years, coding has progressed from a hobby to a critical career skill. Even better for those hobbyists? Employers have shown a willingness to pay a premium for the work of employees with coding and programming ability.

Which of the following, if true, most **strengthens** the argument above?

A Coding is a growing essential skill required in our ever-increasing technological society.
B Coding is a difficult skill to learn and only the most intelligent people can understand it.
C Coding can only be learned through textbooks accessible to all.
D Coding is an engaging skill that everyone is willing to learn.

19 "War is peace, meaning freedom is slavery, meaning ignorance is strength."

If this is true, which of these sentences must also be true?

A If there is no freedom then there is ignorance.
B If there is strength then there is no war.
C If there is slavery then there is no strength.
D If there is no peace then there is no slavery.

20 Water was poured into a container at a constant rate. The graph below shows the depth of water in the container as it was being filled.

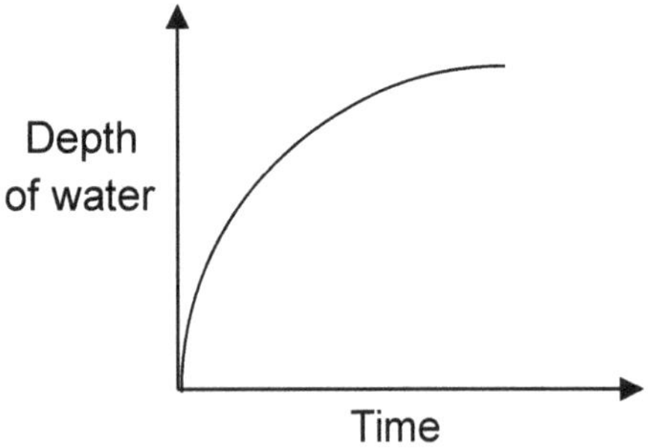

Which of the following containers could have been used?

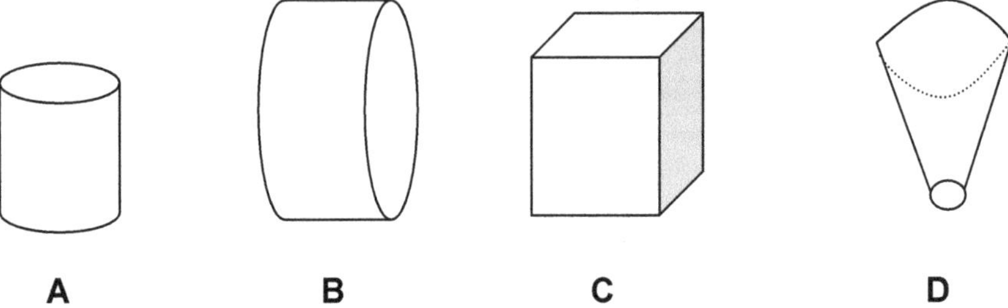

21 There was a secret ballot for becoming the president of Hills Chess Club. The five members of the committee all had two votes and could use one of these votes to vote for themselves. The result of the ballot was:

Committee member	Votes
Aiden	4
Belinda	2
Chris	2
Dianne	1
Eric	1

Dianne knows that each committee member used one of their votes for himself or herself, and she also voted for Chris.

Based on the above information, which one of the following must **not** be true?

A Aiden voted for Belinda
B Chris voted for Belinda
C Belinda voted for Aiden
D Eric voted for Aiden

22 Albert created a banner that displays whether the store is open or closed.

Mel: "Ah, the shop must be closed since that is what the sign is saying."

Albert: "But it is currently 10AM which means they should be open so the sign might be faulty right now."

If the information in the box is true, whose reasoning is correct?

A Albert only.
B Mel only.
C Both Mel and Albert.
D Neither Mel nor Albert.

23 The music program ran in Joshua's school only allow a certain number of students to join the chamber ensemble. Anyone can join however there is a priority placed on students who have played their instrument for more than 4 years.

To try-out for the program, students must perform a musical piece with their chosen instrument. You must also fill in a form explaining why you want to join. If you have played your instrument for more than 4 years you only need to fill out the form.

Despite Joshua only playing the guitar for two years, how come he was still allowed in the ensemble?

A Not enough people who auditioned were able to fit the priority category of the guitar and Joshua was the most outstanding.
B Those who participated as a priority, despite having 4 or more years of experience were not impressive.
C There was an overwhelming number of people who wanted to join the ensemble.
D A lot of people who auditioned dropped out.

24 Ahmed was given 1050ml of rose water in a jug. He wanted to divide it entirely amongst his three sisters, Tanya, Renuka and Tara. It was decided that the youngest sister Tanya should get the smallest portion, which was to be exactly half of Renuka's, while Tara should get the lion's share, i.e. double that of Renuka's.

How much rose water would Renuka get?

A 200 ml
B 250 ml
C 300 ml
D 350 ml

25 Technology affects the way individuals communicate, learn, and think. It helps society and determines how people interact with each other on a daily basis. Technology plays an important role in society today. Technology brought many new methods of electronic communication.

Which of the following, if true, most **weakens** the argument above?

A Technology has negatively impacted society by making knowledge more accessible.
B Communication is ever-evolving and has allowed society to grow in connections.
C Communication and technology have improved people's communication skills.
D Dependence on technology has made individuals less skilled, especially in their communication skills.

26 Work out which of the cubes can be made from the net.

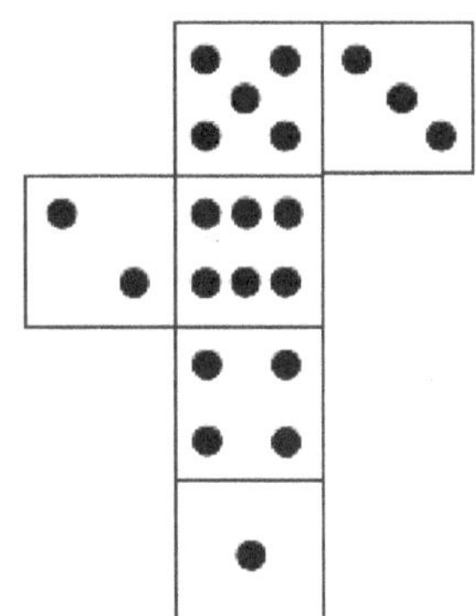

A

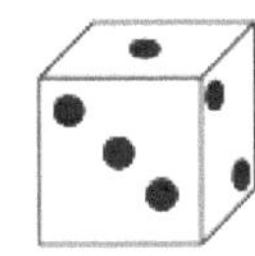

B

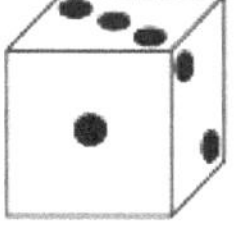

C

D

27 Choose the two shapes that join to form a square.

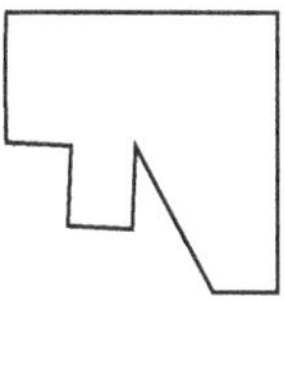

①

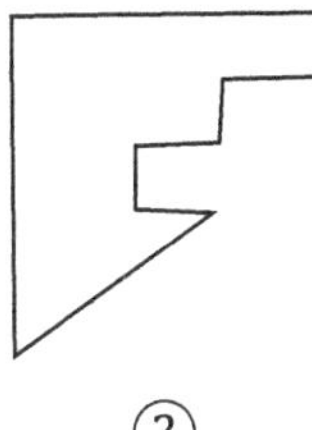

②

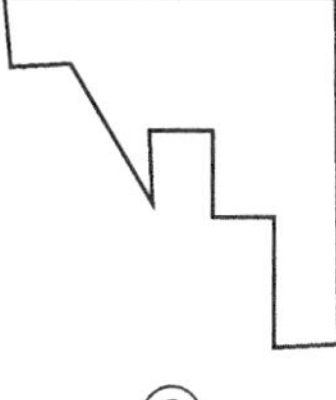

③

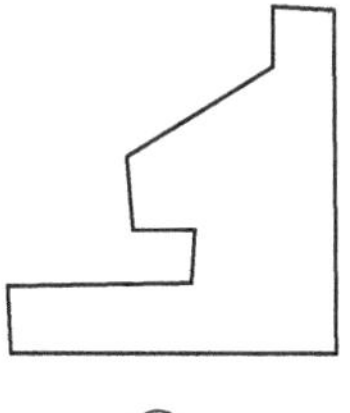

④

A ②, ③
B ①, ③
C ①, ④
D ③, ④

28 Five friends compete with one another to complete the game level the quickest and with the least amount of deaths.

- Ashi and Isabel died the same number of times, three times.
- Guillaume is both second places in speed and number of deaths.
- Nick died five times but finished before Guillaume.
- Luddy finished after Ashi but died the least.
- Isabel finished two before Luddy in terms of speed.

If the following statements are true, only one of the sentences below is true. Which one?

A Isabel finished third place for speed and fifth in deaths.
B Luddy finished the last space in terms of speed.
C Ashi came third in speed.
D Nick died four times.

29 The set menu for a restaurant has different prices per person depending on the total number of people in any group eating there. The prices are shown in the table below.

Group size	Number of courses		
	1	2	3
1 – 6	$10	$12	$17
7 – 12	$9	$11	$16
13 – 20	$8	$10	$15
21+	$7	$9	$14

William has just eaten at the restaurant with 14 of his friends. Everyone had a meal from the set menu: 5 of the group had just 2 courses, while the other 10 had 3 courses.

What was the total price for the meals?

A $170
B $180
C $190
D $200

30 Miran sees two white powders in the kitchen and wanted to bake them, however she cannot taste them. Sugar particles are smaller than salt.

Miran: "I think this is salt since it is finer looking than the other powder."

Which of the following sentences reveals Miran's mistake?

A Sugar can clump up making them look bigger.
B Salt is finer than sugar.
C The white powder is not salt or sugar.
D It depends on what form the sugar and salt are in.

31 There are 480 historical artefacts at a history museum. A fifth are from before the 10th Century, and one eighth were recovered from the Dark Ages between the 11th and 15th inclusive. If two hundred and ten were from after the 19th Century, how many antiques were from between the 16th and 19th Century inclusive?

A 114
B 156
C 237
D 278

32 In a survey of school children who play playground games, everyone who liked 44 homes did not like hopscotch but everyone who liked tag liked hopscotch. Everyone who liked Marco Polo likes 44 homes.

Nin, Johnny, Neil and Vern all took part in the survey.

Based on the information above, which of the following is true?

A If Nin likes hopscotch, then she enjoys 44 homes.
B If Johnny dislikes tag, he likes hopscotch.
C If Neil likes Marco Polo then he enjoys tag.
D If Vern dislikes 44 homes, he likes hopscotch.

33 Will wanted to know within his primary school how many children spoke a second language being: Korean, Mandarin, Cantonese and Hindi. He did a survey of all the students at the school, and found the following:

- There are the same number of students who speak Mandarin and Hindi.
- There are more students who speak Cantonese than Korean.
- More students are fluent in Korean than Hindi.
- All students who speak Mandarin or Cantonese are fluent.

If the above is true, what can be assumed?

A The smallest number of students who speak a second language is Cantonese.
B The least fluent students are those who speak Mandarin.
C The second most fluent speakers are those who speak Korean.
D In the school, most students speak Hindi.

34 Have you been thinking about getting a furry companion? Well, dogs are the right way to go! They are known for being man's best friends with their adorable faces and happy-go-lucky attitudes which fill their owners' lives with so much joy. Did you actually know that dogs can be more than your companion but they also have several benefits to their owners?

Which of the following, if true, most **strengthens** the argument above?

A Dogs love to help their owners by digging holes in the backyard for flowers.
B Dogs help with the health of their owner by reducing their stress.
C Dogs are very high-maintenance pets which will lead to their owners spending a lot of money on them.
D Depending on the type of dog you buy, dogs can be violent at times but also calm.

35 "For last year's words belong to last year's language, the present year's words belong to those who exist now and next year's words await another voice."

If this is true, which of these sentences must **not** be true?

A If any words are spoken five years ago, it is part of last year's language.
B If any words are currently spoken now, it belongs to those who are alive in the current year.
C If any words haven't been spoken yet, then it is a word for next year.
D If any words were spoken three years ago, it is not part of last year's language.

36 A theatre group charged $45 per ticket for the play. Out of the price of each ticket, $27 was used to pay the actors; $7 was used to cover the cost of costumes; $4 was used for miscellaneous expenses, and the rest was profit. If the theatre group sold 120 tickets, how much profit did they make?

A $820
B $840
C $1200
D $1100

37 Sitting next to Seeley, I felt a strange calm about the bees, not my usual reaction to them. The insects thrummed with their own business. They flew past our faces. They got caught in our hair, pulled themselves free and kept flying. They didn't even mind when Seeley gently swept away the top layer of bees to inspect the ones underneath.

What is the underlying assumption made above?

A People generally perceive bees as threatening, being scared of them.
B Seeley is terrified of the bees, not wanting to interact with them.
C Bees will be peaceful as long as you do not interact with them.
D Bees are very busy with caring for their colony they will ignore humans.

38 The Nobel Prize is given out each year to a select few scientists, writers, economists and people working toward peace. From 1901 to 2015, 573 Nobel Prizes have been given out, including household names like Albert Einstein, Marie Curie, Nelson Mandela, Ernest Hemingway, and the International Committee of the Red Cross. It's a long, long history — long enough to be filled with plenty of drama and contention.

Which of the following, if true, most **weakens** the argument above?

A The nominees of the Nobel Prize are nominated by their peers.
B People who have been awarded the Noble Prize can sometimes carry out actions that contradict their prize.
C The Nobel Prize has allowed people to further improve action to their causes in their field.
D Giving out of the prize is a highly publicised event that many around the world tune into.

39 Anne's dance team allows the top three students each term to perform at the end of term performance, to recognise their skills.

Anne: "Since I didn't perform last term but I performed the term before I can't perform this term."

Which of the following sentences reveals Anne's mistake?

A Solo performers are chosen through a list and since she has gone she can't go again.
B The dance team wants to give everyone a fair chance in performing.
C The dance team will allow more than three students to perform, giving everyone a chance.
D Solo performances at the end of the term are not influenced by whether they have performed solo before.

40 Five islands make up the Republic of Bondia.

Island	Area (km^2)	Population
Brosnan	5000	1,200,000
Connery	6000	900,000
Craig	2500	100,000
Dalton	5500	300,000
Lazenby	1000	1,500,000
Total	**20000**	**4,000,000**

Which island contains less than 10% of the population of Bondia, despite accounting for more than 20% of its area?

A Connery
B Craig
C Dalton
D Lazenby

Selective Practice Test Paper
Thinking Skills 7 (Time allowed: 40 min)

INSTRUCTIONS

1. Write your Name on the cover page.
2. There are 40 questions in this paper. For each question there are four possible answers, A, B, C and D. Choose the one correct answer and record your choice on the separate answer sheet. If you make a mistake, erase thoroughly and try again.
3. You will not lose marks for incorrect answers, so you should attempt all 40 questions
4. You must complete the answer sheet within the time limit. There will not be any extra time at the end of the exam to record your answers on the answer sheet.
5. You can use the question paper for working out, but no extra paper is allowed.

Name: ______________________________

1 A cyclist maintains a constant speed for 10 minutes until he reaches a steep downhill. He speeds faster down the hill before taking a break for 10 minutes.

Which graph best represents this situation?

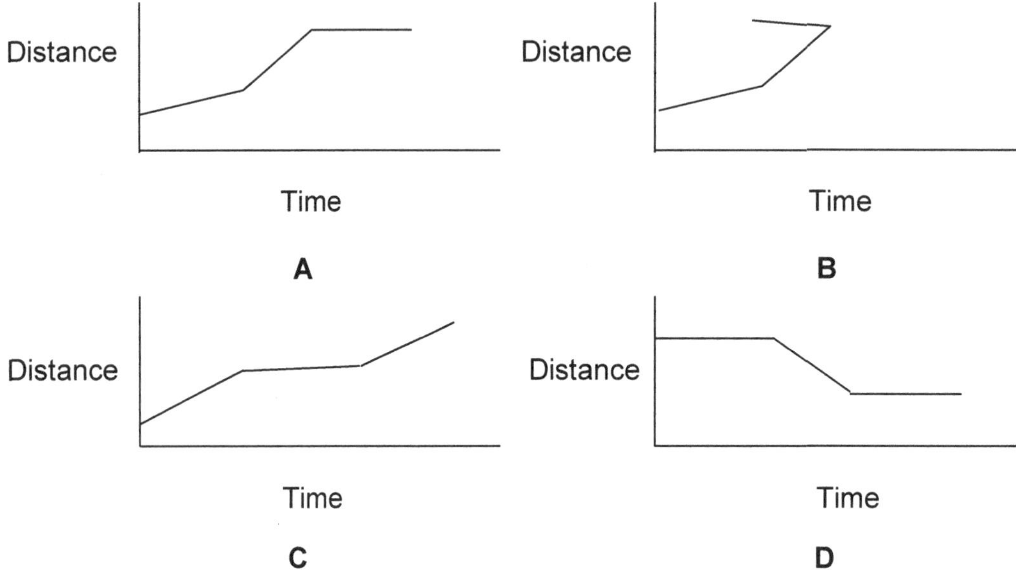

2 Many people in modern society have at least one set of piercings. Despite the abundance of people who have piercings, society still views piercings as unprofessional, meaning that many are rejected from job interviews simply because they have a 'bad image'. People with multiple piercings should remove some of their jewelry to allow for the piercings to heal and close up.

Which one of these statements, if true, most **weakens** the above argument?

A Many people who have piercings can pay for their basic needs and for luxury items through the money they have earned in their jobs
B Piercings are a way that a person can express themselves, similar to painting nails or wearing a style of clothes
C The discrimination against people with multiple piercings is increasing
D Discrimination would not occur if people did not have piercings

3 Politician Jane's opponent, Politician Albert believes that her laws too strongly promote single-family houses and that they should be changed to encourage other housing like apartments.

Jane: Politician Albert believes this, yet he lives in a house in the country. His lifestyle contradicts his own argument, which should therefore not be taken seriously.

Which one of the following sentences shows the mistake that Politician Jane made?

A She does not account for the fact that apartments can be built in the suburbs just as easily as in the centre of the city.
B She fails to mention her own living situation
C She ignores the possibility that Politician Albert may have previously lived in an apartment
D Her discussion of Politician Albert's lifestyle is irrelevant to his argument

4 When I pull string X down, what will happen to the cube and cylinder?

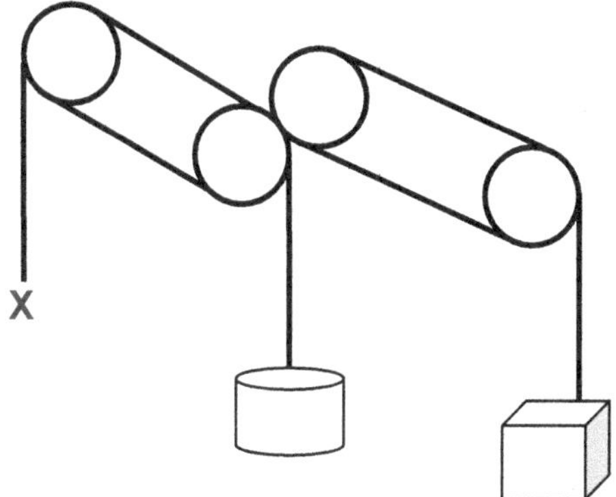

A Cube and cylinder will both go up.
B Cube will go down, cylinder will go up.
C Cube and cylinder will both go down.
D Cylinder will go down, cube will go up.

5

> Kate pressed a button on her device. In the next few minutes, if the device shows any signal then it can successfully detect internet reception. Otherwise, it cannot detect any reception.

Kate: It has been a few minutes already and my device still hasn't reacted. It must not be able to detect internet reception.

Ashley: My device didn't react either when I pressed the button. This area must not have any internet reception at all.

If the information in the box is true, whose reasoning is correct?

A Kate only
B Ashley only
C Both Kate and Ashley
D Neither Kate nor Ashley

6 The amount of a certain medicine required by a baby depends on its weight, as shown in the table below.

Weight (kg)	Amount of medicine (ml)
2.5 – 3.5	3.0
3.5 – 5.0	4.0
5.0 – 6.5	4.5
6.5 – 8.0	5.0

Four babies were weighed and given the correct amount of medicine in October and again in January.

Which baby required the greatest increase in the amount of medicine from October to January?

	Weight in October (kg)	Weight in January (kg)
A	6.0	7.0
B	3.0	4.0
C	4.0	6.0
D	7.0	8.0

7 The Swedish chemist and engineer Alfred Nobel invented dynamite is well known for his invention becoming rich and being known as the 'Merchant of Death' as it led to an increased loss of life. At his death in 1896 he did something unusual, bequeathing about $260 million to create prizes to reward various scientific and cultural advances produced by people or organizations anywhere in the world. Thus, the Nobel Prizes were born.

What is the underlying assumption made above?

A The invention of dynamite was not a new creation.
B Alfred Nobel gave himself the title of the 'Merchant of Death' due to the effectiveness of dynamite at causing death.
C Sweden creates many talented Noble Prize recipients, highlighting the effective nature of their schooling system.
D The Nobel Prize was created so that Nobel's name would have a positive connotation.

8 Students have found that drinking bottled spring water can lead to improved performance in the workplace over regular tap water. It is believed that the minerals in the water energises and refresh the individual's body and mind. For this reason, it would be beneficial for businesses to buy bottled spring water for their employees to drink throughout the working day.

Which one of these statements, if true, most **weakens** the above argument?

A Bottled spring water has minerals that tap water does not have
B Bottled spring water has all the minerals that tap water has, plus more
C The bottled spring water and the tap water both draw their water from the exact same source
D If workers are refreshed, their minds would be more focused on the work they need to complete

9

> Technology companies should try to make their handheld devices more suitable for the older generation. Technology companies around the world have not taken the initiative to do this, therefore, it could greatly benefit the companies that do.

Which one of the following sentences summarises the main conclusion to the above argument?

A By spending money on handheld devices, technology companies will earn more money

B Technology companies should create new devices to prevent difficulties faced by elderly buyers

C If the technology companies hire more workers to upgrade the handheld devices, they could have a decrease in profit

D Technology companies should accommodate the older generation, which may greatly benefit them

10 The symbols at 'A' are transformed into the symbol at 'B' by following the actions in the order they are given in the 'Rule' columns.

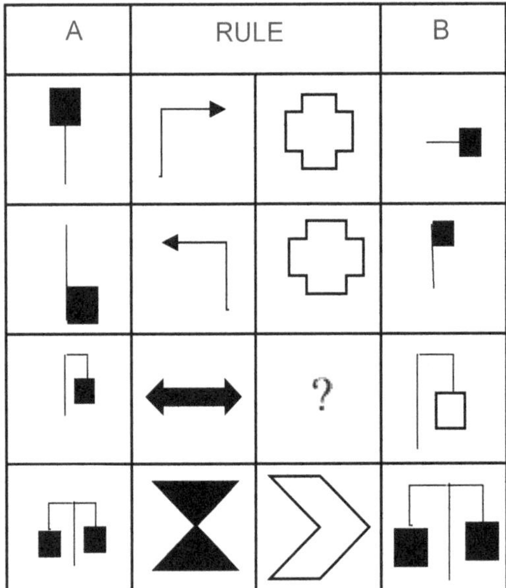

What is the missing rule?

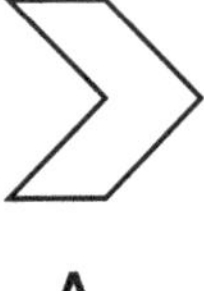

A

B

C

D

11

> The three languages, Sanshi, Sanskari and Shelo are quite similar to each other and have a lot of common words. For example, "Jenu" means sun in all three languages.
>
> Any word that is the same in Sanshi and Shelo is also the same in Sanskari
>
> Sanskari and Shelo have a lot of words in common, but never words for greetings. Words for greetings are always different.

Patrick: "If a word is the same in Sanshi and Shelo, it can't be a greeting

Katy: "If a word is the same in Sanshi and Sanskari, it can't be a greeting

If the information in the box is true, whose reasoning is correct?

A Patrick only
B Katy only
C Both Patrick and Katy
D Neither Patrick nor Katy

12 Beck and Jesse wanted to find out which sport was the most popular at their school, between volleyball, soccer or cricket. They did a survey of all the students at the school and found the following:

- Everyone who liked volleyball also liked cricket
- Some people liked both cricket and soccer
- No one liked both soccer and volleyball
- There were more people who only liked cricket than people who only liked soccer

Using the information above, what was the most popular sport?

A Volleyball
B Cricket
C Soccer
D Tied between cricket and volleyball

Questions 13 and 14 refer to the following information.

A tile is made up of equilateral triangles.

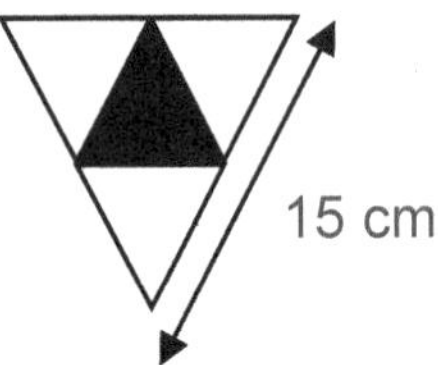

The tile is tessellated to fill this parallelogram.

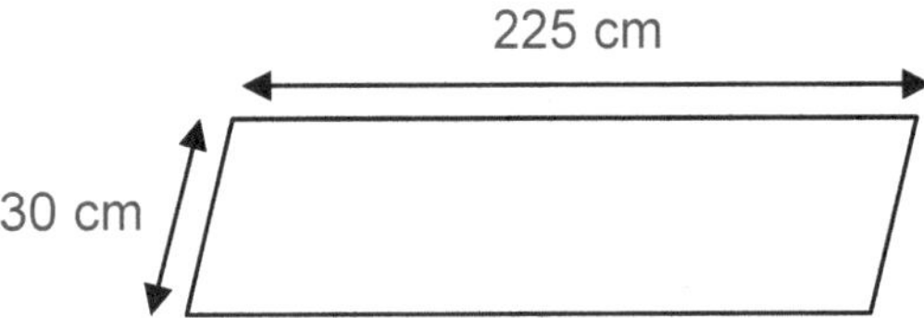

13 How many tiles are needed to fill the parallelogram?

A 10
B 20
C 30
D 40

14 If each tile is hypothetically 36 cm^2 in area, what area is covered by the black triangles?

A 225 cm^2
B 270 cm^2
C 300 cm^2
D 315 cm^2

15 One of the best things about fiction is that writers do not have to stick to the same rules as our own universe. While the real world is restricted by the rules of physics, such as gravity, a made-up world does not have to have the same rules. Although a made-up world does not have to have the rules of the real world, there may also be rules made within the make-believe world which makes the world reasonable.

Which one of these statements best concludes the passage above?

A A make-believe world must always have rules of its own
B An author essentially has lots of flexibility around the rules of their world
C If the author does not make their world bizarre, it would not be entertaining
D Stories about the real world cannot be as entertaining as made-up worlds

16

> Insurance statistics show that more cars with alarms or other antitheft devices are stolen or broken into each year than cars without these devices or alarms.

Sarah: "Antitheft devices, like alarms, do not protect cars against thieves at all."

Which one of the following sentences shows the mistake Sarah has made?

A She assumes that antitheft devices make it easier for thieves to break in
B She ignores the fact that insurance statistics are generally unrepresentative
C She ignores the potential for there to be a much higher number of cars with antitheft devices than cars without them
D She assumes that the main purpose of antitheft devices is to protect cars against thieves

17 Ducks are a type of bird and they quack. Chickens are also a type of bird, but they do not quack. Therefore, chickens and ducks are not the same breed of birds.

Which of the following most closely parallels the reasoning in the above argument?

A Child A's name is Alex. Child B's name is also Alex. Since Child A is male and Child B is female, Alex is both a male and female name.
B Water bills on average cost $100 per month. Electricity bills on average cost $200 per month. Therefore, the electricity bill costs 2 times the water bill.
C The current temperature in NSW is 29 degrees Celsius. The temperature in SA is also 29 degrees Celsius. Therefore, both states are in Australia.
D Soft drinks are a liquid that are flavoured. Water is also a liquid, but it does not have a flavour. Therefore, soft drinks and water are not the same type of liquids.

18

> "When girls are educated in girls high schools, they tend to do better academically than girls who attend co-educational high schools."

Alayna: My friend achieved higher grades than any other woman in her first year at the university. Therefore, she was probably educated at a girls high school.

Lizzie: My friend achieved a higher score than her friends in other schools. Therefore, she probably attended a co-educational high school.

If the information in the box is true, whose reasoning is correct?

A Alayna only
B Lizzie only
C Both Alayna and Lizzie
D Neither Alayna nor Lizzie

19

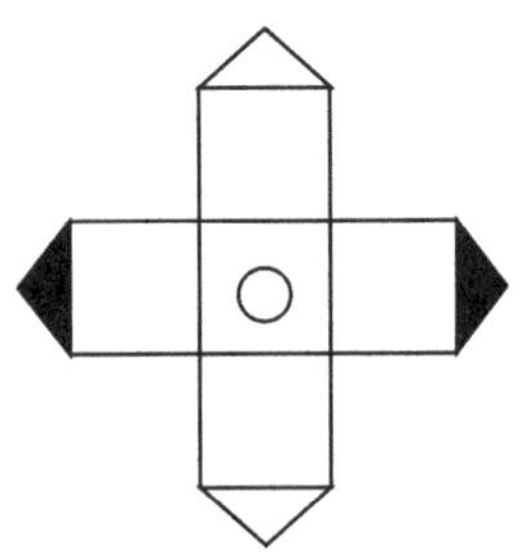

Which of the following cubes can be formed by folding the net shown above?

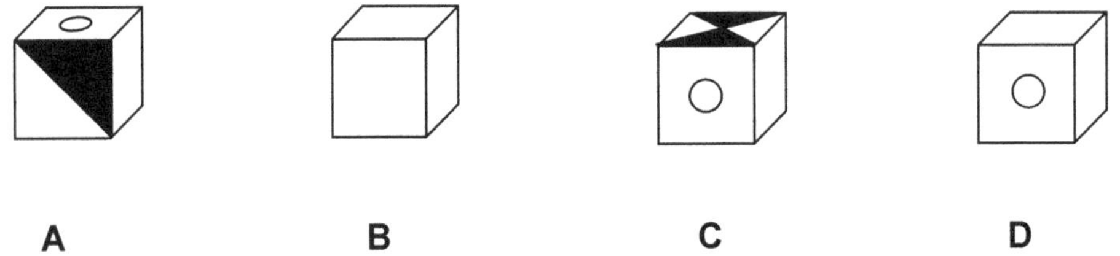

20 The rate of a certain crime in major cities has been increasing every year. The number of armed police officers has also increased every year. The government is now debating spending money on a new special taskforce for these certain types of crimes. Several ex-chiefs of police believe that this will be very beneficial. However, we can see from the statistics that the increase in the number of armed police officers is rising at the same time as the amount of specific crime. A new taskforce would just add to the problem rather than solve it.

Which one of these statements, if true, would most **weaken** the above argument?

A Ex-chiefs have a lot of experience, thus their opinion is very valuable
B Officers in the special taskforce will have similar skills to regular police officers
C The increasing number of armed police officers is not related to the increasing number of the certain crime committed
D The exact number of crimes committed is unknown

21 A group of scientists is conducting a research study on the health effects of food irradiation. They have discovered that there is no evidence that challenges the safety of their practice.

Scientist: Since there is no evidence that shows food irradiation is unsafe, the public can remain satisfied that food irradiation is definitely a safe practice.

Which of the following shows the mistake that the scientist has made?

A A lack of evidence that challenges food irradiation cannot be used as definitive evidence for the safety of food irradiation
B Food irradiation is a practice that has been known for centuries, so the study was not needed at all
C She has ignored the health benefits of food irradiation, namely the destruction of harmful microbes
D She must consider the reactions of the public to this health announcement before concluding that it is a safe practice

22 The result of competition on different railway routes can result in the prices of tickets seeming to be almost random. People are allowed to use more than one ticket to make a journey, so long as the end of one is the start of the next.

The prices of tickets for different journeys are shown below.

KVB			
$3	**Linfield**		
$7	$2	**Marrickville**	
$11	$6	$5	**North beach**

What is the cheapest total fare that can be used to get from KVB to North beach?

A $7
B $8
C $9
D $10

23

> Some of the great sea-mammals, such as the beluga whale, have brains larder than humans. It is a fact that organs do not grow or remain large unless they are used, meaning that is they are not used, they shrink or even disappear. Therefore, we can conclude that the beluga whale makes intelligent use of their brain, perhaps at thought levels well beyond our understanding.

Which one of the following, if true, would **weaken** the above argument?

A Beluga whale's intelligence is a kind of intelligence that humans cannot understand
B There are many other sea-mammals that have brains larger than beluga whales
C Beluga whales can do many things that humans cannot do
D Larger brains can be used for purposes not related to intelligence

24 "Dinosaurs were reptiles. Hence, scientists believed that, like all reptiles today, dinosaurs were cold-blooded. It has been discovered that some dinosaurs were warm-blooded."

1. Dinosaurs may not have all been reptiles
2. Some reptiles may be warm-blooded

If the quoted statement is true, which reasoning above shows the potential to be correct?

A 1
B 2
C Both 1 and 2
D Neither 1 nor 2

25 Year 5 at a certain school has 1000 students. Each year, as children move on to the next grade up, the number of new students in Year 5 decreases by 20%. If each year, 10 students have to repeat Year 5, how many students will there be in the grade in 2 years time?

A 658
B 728
C 444
D 634

26 In a high-speed police chase, police drivers sometimes lose sight of the car they are chasing. However, there is an easy way to find the car again. All they must do is take the first left, and then the first left again. Pursued drivers are likely to keep taking turns as they come up, as this seems indistinctively like the best way to lose someone who is following them. Therefore, taking a couple of left turns will result in having sight of the criminal again.

Which one of these statements, if true, most **strengthens** the above argument?

A Criminals tend to not turn right, as this involves waiting and checking for oncoming traffic which takes too long
B The criminal's car will blend in with the rest of the cars on the road
C If the criminal takes two left turns, the police should make a U-turn, then turn right to meet the criminals at an intersection
D Police cars are usually faster than normal cars, so police drivers will not lose sight of the criminals' cars

27

The Summer Festival is an annual event that features dances, songs, DJs, instrumentals and a party at the end. It is always a smash hit, with the places being filled all the time. In order to obtain a place, tickets must be bought before Wednesday and only the first 200 tickets bought will be given a space. A further limited 50 tickets will be released on Friday to those who missed out, but at a higher price.

Brendon: "I bought a ticket as soon as they got released, I will be guaranteed a place!"

Akash: "I can only buy a ticket on Saturday, as I'm waiting for funds to get transferred, I can still make it"

If the information in the box is true, whose reasoning is correct?

A Brendon only
B Both Brendon and Akash
C Akash only
D Neither Brendon nor Akash

28 Choose the graph which shows a hot summer day which is cooled by a storm but then starts to heat up again.

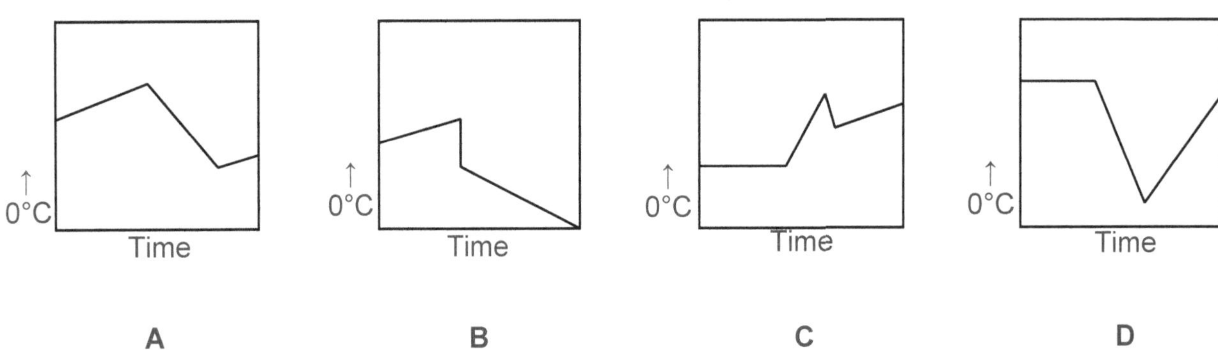

29 Keeping heat from leaving houses helps people to save on heating bills. However, it can be expensive for families to pay for the proper equipment needed to keep the heat in, especially if their house already has older equipment installed. Since lower heating bills benefit the environment, the government should lower the amount of tax that households and landlords need to pay so they can buy equipment to keep the heat in.

What is the major assumption made in doing this?

A Families do not want better equipment for their houses
B The majority of households and landlords refuse to buy better equipment because of financial reasons
C The government does not care about benefitting the environment
D Properly caring for the house is not a big concern of households and landlords

30 Below shows the earnings across different companies between the years 2018 to 2021.

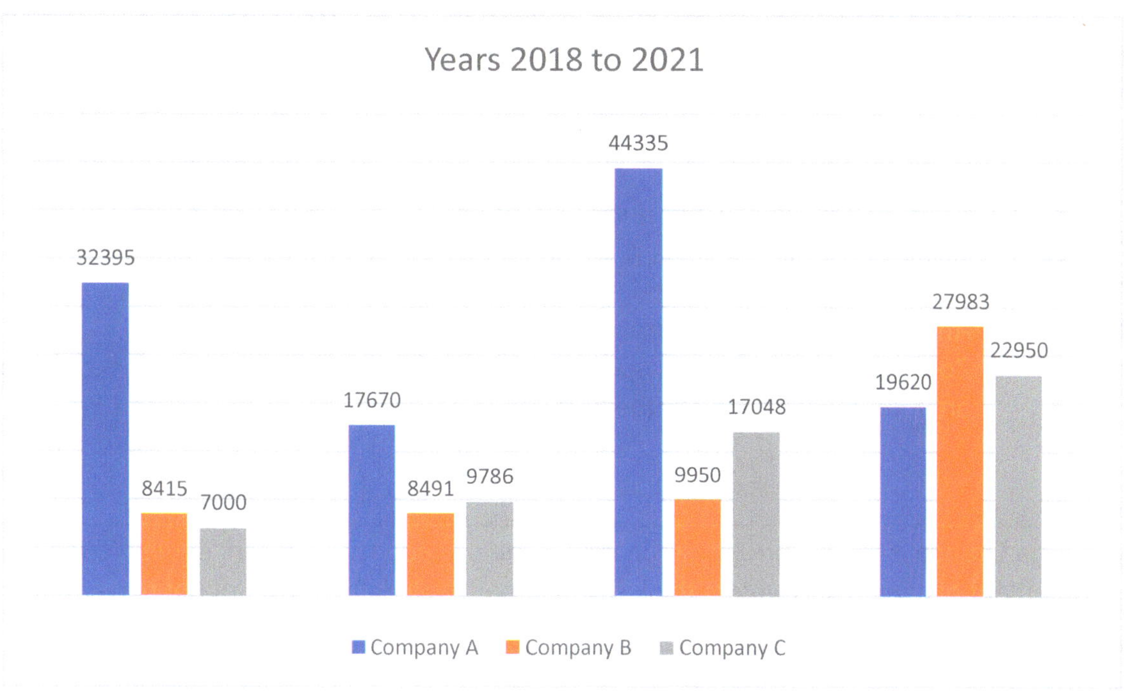

Work out the total earnings for Company B

A 48834
B 50340
C 54839
D 60123

31 According to the United States Agency for International Development (USAID), food security means having, at all times, both physical and economic access to sufficient food to meet dietary needs for a productive and healthy life. Put more simply, families can afford and obtain enough nutritious food. A family is food secure when its members do not live in hunger or fear of hunger. Food security is experienced all around the world.

Which of the following, if true, most **strengthens** the argument above?

A Food security has been solved by the United Nations.
B Food security is least needed in nations that do not have enough resources to tackle.
C Food security is felt all around the world, including in developed nations like America.
D Food security is simple to achieve and has been planned out.

32 "Zoos are unsuitable places for animals to live in. People visit zoos to learn about animal behaviour, but the animals they see are likely to be behaving in abnormal ways because of the cramped and unnatural conditions in which they are kept. Zoos should be closed, and the money should instead be spent on the protection of natural habitats."

Which one of these statements, if true, most **weakens** the above argument?

A Children enjoy looking at animals in zoos
B Animals in zoos, like lions and cheetahs, cannot run freely in their closed areas and therefore do not have enough physical activity to stay healthy
C Animals in zoos are generally less happy than animals in the wild
D Zoos enable endangered species to survive and breed in a safe location before they are then re-introduced to the wild

33 The Orange Party is currently in charge of the city council. A recent survey found that 71 percent of compulsory voters think that this party will definitely be out of power after next year's city council elections.

Bob: "Due to this survey, the voters would all happily welcome the defeat of the Orange Party."

Lola: "Hold on a second Bob. Just because these voters think that the Orange Party will lose, that does not mean that they will actually vote in the election."

If the information in the box is true, whose reasoning is correct?

A Bob only
B Lola only
C Both Bob and Lola
D Neither Bob nor Lola

34 Matchsticks are used to create the shapes for the pattern below.

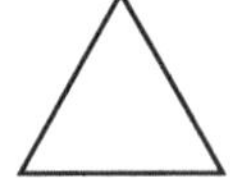
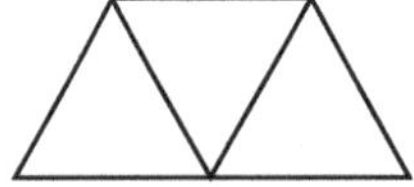
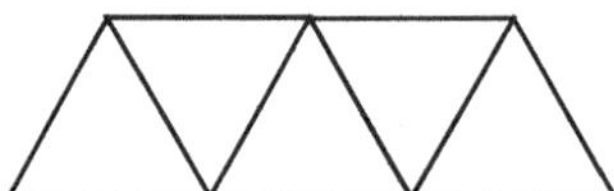

How many matchsticks will be needed to form the sixth shape?

A 21
B 23
C 25
D 27

35 **Charlie:** "I tried a speed-reading course and read a book in two hours. It's about travelling into another universe."

Charlie's comment draws the attention of many who doubt the effectiveness of speed-reading techniques. These techniques usually involve moving your finger smoothly and quickly along lines of text and training your eyes to follow, thus preventing your eyes from going back over words you have already read. There have been reports of readers achieving incredible speeds using these techniques, but such achievements are of limited benefit to many readers, particularly students, who must gain a deep understanding of what they read.

Which one of these statements, if true, most **weakens** the above argument?

A If a student reads too fast, they will not be able to understand the deeper messages that a book is trying to convey
B Students, after the comment, stated that they find the contents of a book better if they read it quickly
C People who speed-read will quickly forget the contents of a book
D Speed-reading does not make you a lot faster than regular reading speeds

36 In a particular country, all citizens are either pure vegetarians or non-vegetarians.

Tribe S is fully vegetarian. People from Tribe Z are mainly vegetarians but eat chicken.

Which of the following statements **MUST** be true?

A Tribe Z is vegetarian
B There are mostly vegetarians in this country
C Tribe Z is probably not allowed to eat fish
D None of the above

37 Adding one block at a time, it took 20 seconds to put this solid P together.

Working at the same rate choose the length of time needed to put solid S together.

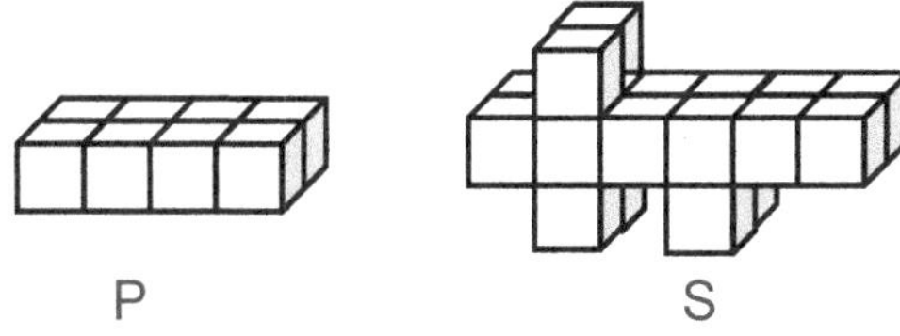

A 35 seconds
B 40 seconds
C 45 seconds
D 50 seconds

38

> If you compare darts to any sport currently performed at the Olympics, you will see that they differ greatly in terms of skill and energy required to play the sport. Track, boxing, gymnastics, volleyball and any other Olympic sport you can think of require years of training, sacrifice, focus and complete dedication to complete at a world-class level. Darts players, on the other hand, smoke and drink between turns and do not have a competitive drive to win whilst playing.

Which of the following statements best concludes the above passage?

A Darts is a relaxing social sport unlike other competitive sports seen in the Olympics
B Darts is like any other sport played at the Olympics in all aspects
C Darts should not be a sport at all, due to the lack of dedication needed
D Olympic sports are the best sports available for an individual to choose from

39 In tennis, the world's fastest serve travels at a speed of 253km/h, which is equivalent to 70m/s. When the server hits the ball, they are approximately 24 metres away from the opponent, which means that the opponent has less than half a second to react to the ball and return the ball. According to scientists, this is impossible as there is simply not enough time for the necessary thought processes and muscle responses to occur, yet this is exactly what happens. This just shows that there are situations that science cannot explain due to its own limitations.

Which one of these bests **strengthens** the argument above?

A There have been many cases where humans have been able to surpass the limits and expectations placed upon them by science
B Science is never incorrect when evidence backs up the initial beliefs
C These are points that a server gains through hitting the ball so fast that the opponent cannot react or return the ball
D In a double game, the pairs stand on opposite sides of a field to cover more area

40 Following graph shows the number of births and deaths recorded during each year, over a seven-year period on an island. The total population at the start of the seven-year period was 1000 people.

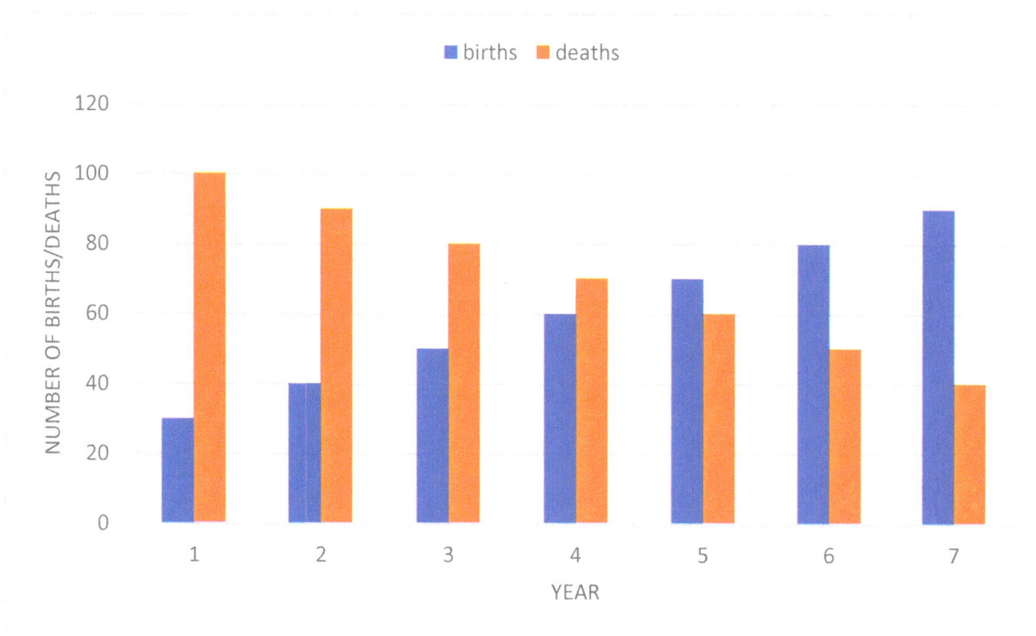

Assuming there is not any immigration or emigration on the island, which of the following shows the total population over the seven-year period?

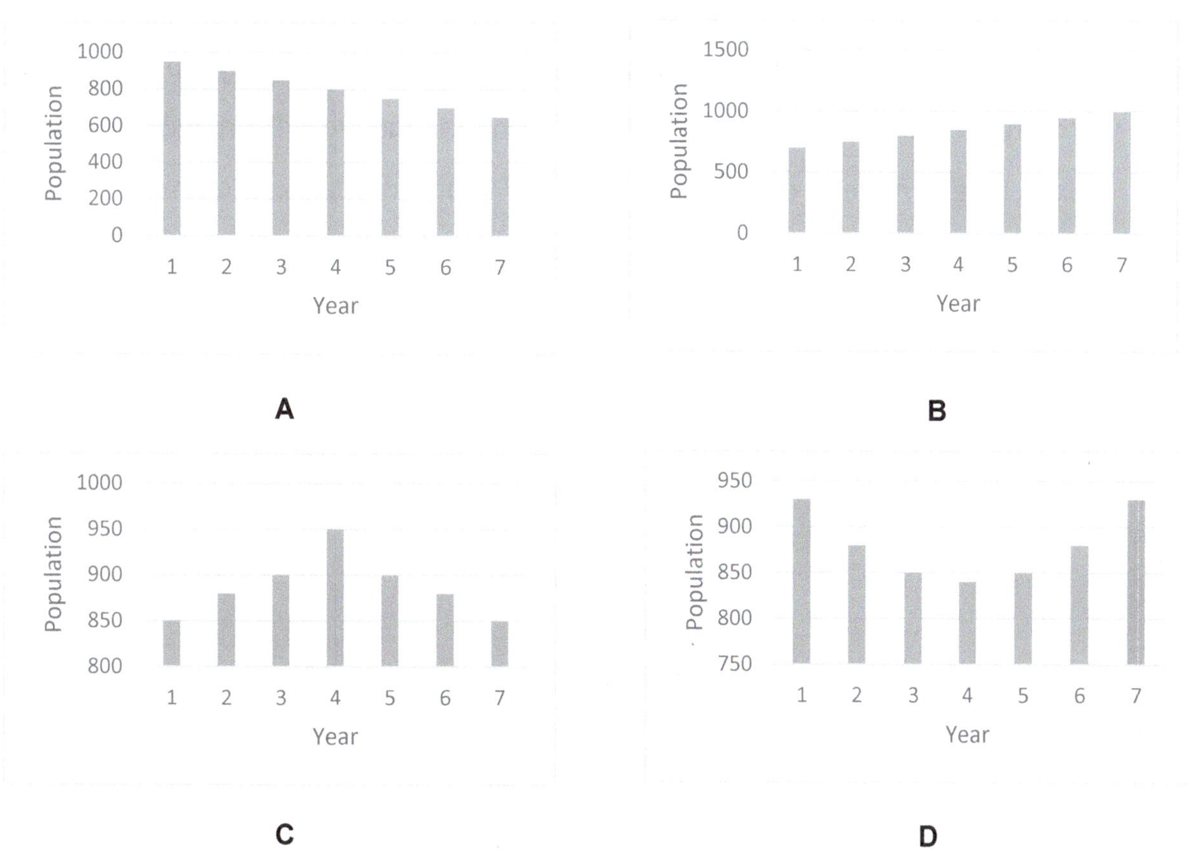

Selective Practice Test Paper
Thinking Skills 8 (Time allowed: 40 min)

INSTRUCTIONS

1 Write your Name on the cover page.
2 There are 40 questions in this paper. For each question there are four possible answers, A, B, C and D. Choose the one correct answer and record your choice on the separate answer sheet. If you make a mistake, erase thoroughly and try again.
3 You will not lose marks for incorrect answers, so you should attempt all 40 questions
4 You must complete the answer sheet within the time limit. There will not be any extra time at the end of the exam to record your answers on the answer sheet.
5 You can use the question paper for working out, but no extra paper is allowed.

Name: ______________________________

1 In today's society social networking sites such as Facebook and Twitter play a huge part in our lives. These websites are fantastic for communicating with friends and family that we don't often see. They are a great way of connecting with new people who have the same interests as you.

Which of the statements, if true, most **strengthens** the above argument?

A They are also a great way to make new friends or find old ones.
B Social media is distracting
C Facebook and Twitter are the two most famous social networking sites
D Social media has its negatives and disadvantages

2

Whenever Leslie craves waffles, she goes to the local diner for breakfast. And whenever she finishes eating at the local diner, she always visits the local markets on the way home.

Tom: "I saw Leslie at the local markets last weekend, so she must have been at the local diner that same day."

Andy: "I bumped into Leslie at the local diner yesterday, so she must have gone to the markets after that."

If the information in the box is correct, whose reasoning is correct?

A Tom Only
B Andy Only
C Neither of them
D Both of them

3 A survey has been carried out of the methods of transport to school used by pupils. The results, broken down by year group, are shown below.

	Year 2	Year 3	Year 4	Year 5	Total
Car	20	15	15	10	60
Scooter	10	10	15	15	50
Bicycle	3	2	5	10	17
Walk	30	33	25	25	113
Total	60	60	60	60	240

One of the individual entries in the above table has been typed incorrectly, although the marginal totals are correct. Which value is wrong?

A 2
B 3
C 5
D 33

4 I am planning to buy a new laptop. The following table shows the specifications and the prices of my shortlist.

laptop	Processor speed (GHz)	Memory (GB)	Storage (GB)	Graphics card memory (GB)	Screen size (inches)	Price ($)
HP	2.7	4	500	2	15.0	600
ASUS	2.8	8	1000	4	14.0	850
DELL	2.5	4	750	6	15.0	500
SAMSUNG	2.8	8	1000	6	17.0	700

In terms of storage, the operating system and my files take up 300 GB. I would also like a laptop with a screen size of at least 15 inches. I am looking for the cheapest laptop that can run the following game:

MINIMUM SYSTEM REQUIREMENTS OF GAME				
game	Processor speed (GHz)	Memory (GB)	Storage (GB)	Graphics card memory (GB)
StarCraft	2.5	6	60	4

Which laptop should I buy?

A HP
B ASUS
C DELL
D SAMSUNG

5 There has been considerable publicity regarding the dangers of exposure to the sun. People who lie on the beach in order to get a tan are encouraged to put on high factor sun creams to reduce the risk of skin cancer. However, we should remember that sunshine provides us with Vitamin D, and this is important in keeping our bones strong and in helping to protect us against various diseases. Sun protection creams considerably reduce the body's ability to make Vitamin D. In consequence we must ensure that we have frequent exposure to the sun for the sake of our health.

Which one of the following is the best statement of the **flaw** in the above argument?

A The author fails to show that, though Vitamin D is necessary for health, sunshine isn't the only source of it.
B The author fails to specify how frequent exposure to the sun could be beneficial to our health.
C The author's conclusion is inconsistent with their advice about the dangers of exposure to the sun.
D The author does not explain why Vitamin D is the main factor in determining our health.

6 The parasite which causes malaria lives in red blood cells which die in a person's body after 120 days. Since the parasite cannot travel to any new red blood cells, any fever that develops in a person for more than 120 days after that person has moved to a malaria-free location is not due to the malarial parasite.

Which one of these statements, if true, most **weakens** the above argument?

A In some cases, the parasite that causes malarial fevers can travel to other types of cells which die less often in a person's body than red blood cells
B The fever caused by the malarial parasite is similar to flu fevers, in that it causes the same bodily responses
C Many symptoms of malaria other than the fever can reappear within 120 days after medication has stopped being taken
D In any location which has malarial parasites there are people who may be immune to malaria

7

The Federal Government spent an estimated $24.8 Billion dollars on improving and building new roads and infrastructure around the country. This was said to reduce congestion and prepare for the future growth, reducing travel times and making commutes much smoother. The general public so far, in the past 2 months, have reported no difference in their commute.

Hector: "The roads and infrastructure project is a complete waste of taxpayers' money and funds. They should instead make better use of funds and improve the livelihoods of citizens"

Which one of the following sentences shows the mistake Hector has made?

A Over time, when congestion grows dramatically, commuters will begin to appreciate the projects.
B The Federal Government makes accurate decisions based on certified and qualified data.
C Such large-scale projects take lots of time for planning and development, as such are very critical for the function of the nation.
D The projects put the country on a global scale which has a long term positive impact

Questions 8 and 9 use the following information.

These are three views of the same cube.

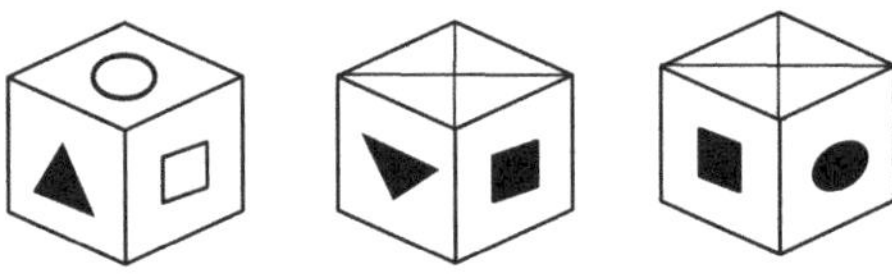

8 What shape is on the face opposite ■ ?

9 Choose the net for the cube.

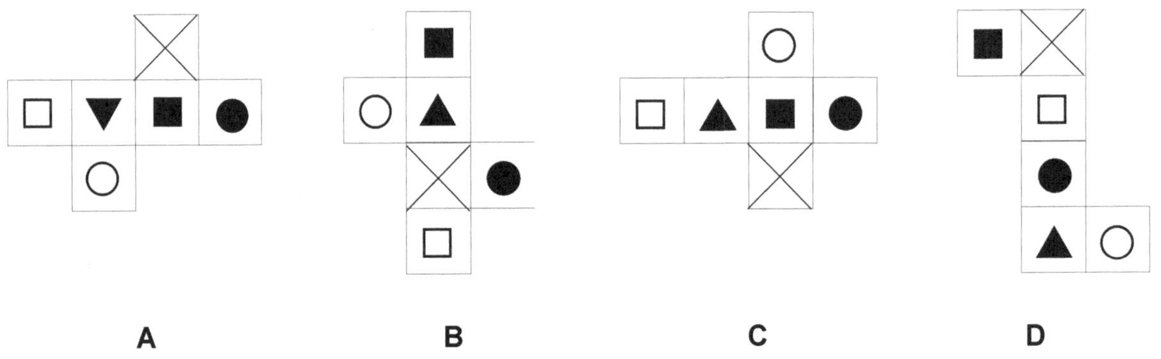

10 The refugee crisis seemed to reach a peak in the middle of this decade. Thousands of civilians from war-torn countries in the Middle East have fled to Europe to avoid violence and poverty. However, this has put a lot of pressure on public services in Europe. Rather than paying refugees to live in Europe, we should instead focus on stopping wars and conflicts in the Middle East so that these refugees can return to their homes.

Which one of these would **strengthen** the above argument?

A When the society in Europe collapses, there would be more criminal acts which can put the refugees in danger in their new home
B Public services in Europe are becoming more developed and widespread
C Wars and conflicts will constantly break out in the Middle East due to ongoing political tensions between the countries
D The refugees would be too afraid to return to their homes in the Middle East even if the violence has been solved

11 If Andy does not get up on time, he will miss his bus.
If he misses the bus, he cannot get to school.
If he does not get to school, he will not receive his award at assembly.

If the above statements are correct, which one of the following is **not** possible?

A Andy missed his bus and received his award at the assembly
B Andy missed the bus because he did not get up on time
C Andy did not get to school because he did not get up on time
D Andy did not sleep well, so he did not get up on time

12 A square piece of paper has been folded in the order shown below. After that, pieces of different shapes have been cut out. Which figure shows the paper when it is opened up?

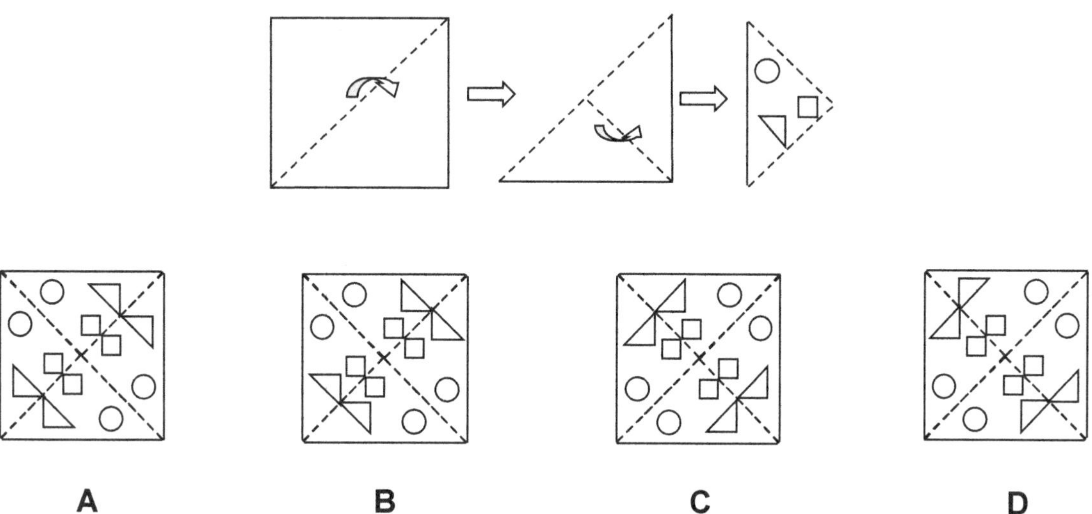

13 Which of the views is **not** relevant to the following shape?

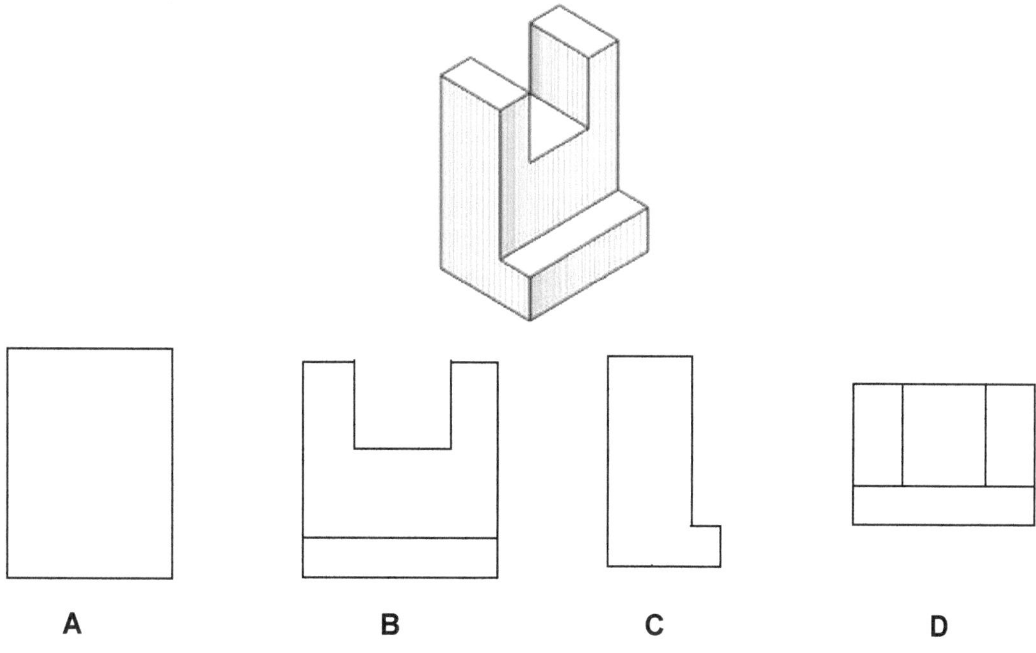

14 In a survey, everyone who liked Twisties liked Cheezels. Everyone who liked Cheezels liked Chips, but no one who liked Cheezels liked Crackers.

Danny, Alan, Kevin and Lassie all took part in the survey.

Based on the above information, which one of the following must be true?

A If Danny likes Chips, he also likes Cheezels
B If Alan does not like Crackers, she does not like Chips
C If Lassie likes Twisties, she does not like Crackers
D If Kevin does not like Twisties, he does not like Cheezels

15 A company gives a bonus to all of its salespeople who show a greater percentage increase in sales from year 2 to year 3 than they did from year 1 to year 2. Four salespeople's sales are shown in the graphs below.

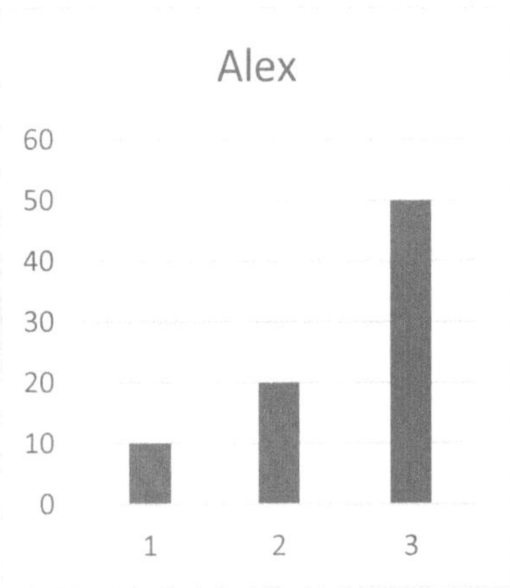

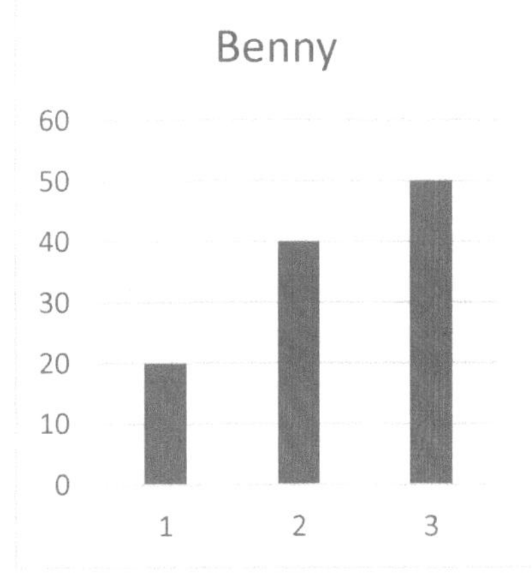

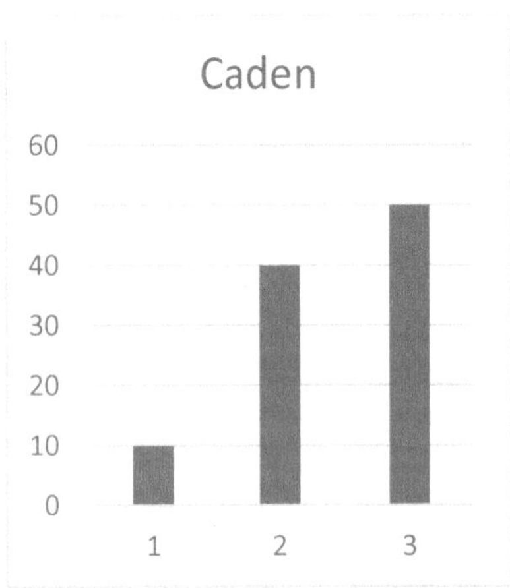

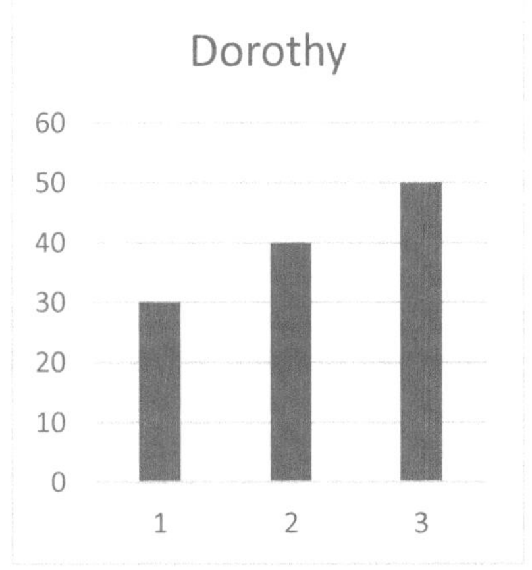

Which employee does receive a bonus?

A Alex
B Benny
C Caden
D Dorothy

16 Next time you feel the flu coming on, you should think twice before reaching for painkillers because they could do more harm than good by increasing the transmission of flu. Obviously, painkillers can make you feel better by reducing muscle pains and headaches, but they also lower fever. Fever is thought to be an antiviral weapon, because many viruses find it hard to replicate at temperatures higher than the normal human body temperature. Some studies have shown that lowering fever can prolong viral infections and increase the amount of the virus that can be passed on to others.

Which one of the following, if true, **strengthens** the above argument?

A Overuse of painkillers can reduce their effectiveness in curing headaches.
B The most effective defense against the flu is an annual anti-flu injection.
C The studies of the effect of lowering fever were carried out on animals, not humans.
D Taking painkillers increases the likelihood that flu sufferers will return to work while still infectious.

17 Jessica lives in Ashfield and wants to go by bus to Randwick to arrive before 16:00 to meet her friend. On the way, she wants to stop in Burwood for at least 40 minutes to do some shopping.

Bus Timetable					
ASHFIELD	13:08	13:17	14:10	14:32	14:42
BURWOOD	13:40	13:50	14:30	15:02	15:18
CAMPSIE	14:13	14:28	14:58	15:23	15:50
HURSTVILLE	14:28	14:50	15:16	15:38	16:06
RANDWICK	14:50	15:12	15:38	15:56	16:20

Which is the latest bus she can catch that will let her do her shopping and meet her friend on time?

A 13:08
B 13:17
C 14:10
D 14:32

18

> The Grand Prix is held once a year. There are three ways to qualify:
>
> - Any driver that wins their nationals qualifies automatically
> - Last year's champion qualifies automatically (as long as they competed in their nationals)
> - One driver can qualify as a 'wild card': This driver is chosen randomly from all the nationals who failed to qualify otherwise
>
> Becky and Jacob are trying to qualify for this year's Grand Prix

Becky: "I won the championship last year, but because of problems with my car I could not compete in the nationals. I still qualify"

Jacob: "I came second in my nationals, there's no chance I can qualify for the Grand Prix"

If the information in the box is true, whose reasoning is correct?

A Jacob only
B Becky only
C Neither Becky nor Jacob
D Both Becky and Jacob

19 The table below shows the list of activities available during the school holidays. Each child from a particular family must take a maximum of one class per day. It can be either in the morning or afternoon.

	Monday	*Tuesday*	*Wednesday*	*Thursday*	*Friday*
Morning	Egg and spoon races	Painting	Egg and spoon races	Ice skating	Egg and spoon races
	Painting	Ice skating	Tennis	Tennis	Bicycle riding
	Colouring	Colouring	Colouring	Colouring	Colouring
Afternoon	Bicycle riding	Bicycle riding	Hiking	Hiking	Hiking
	Athletics	Swimming	Bicycle riding	Bicycle riding	Swimming
	Tennis	Egg and spoon races	Ice skating	Painting	Painting

Zoe has chosen the activities: colouring, painting, hiking, swimming and athletics.

In order to have Friday afternoon free for going to the beach, on which day must she do painting?

A Monday
B Tuesday
C Wednesday
D Thursday

20 Success in modern countries is measured by the quantity of possessions one has. A lack of possessions means one is judged to be unsuccessful. Those people with few possessions therefore must feel a strong sense of failure.

Which one of the following is an underlying assumption of the above argument?

A People who do not possess a lot of items are failures
B People who are successful will buy more and people who are less successful will buy less
C Success is very important to people in modern society
D The citizens of America are right to believe that success can be measured through possessions

21 Mr Lee would like to investigate whether eating almonds improve his students' marks. He decides to conduct an experiment.

He splits his class into two equal groups of 10 each, Group A and Group B. For one whole term, Group A has almonds everyday as part of their diet. Group B eats their normal diet, without almonds.

After a term, Mr Lee gives the whole class a test. On average, students who ate almonds as part of their diet, scored higher than the students who did not.

Mr Lee: "So it's true! Eating almonds does improve a student's marks!"

Which one of the following sentences shows the mistake Mr Lee has made?

A Students in Group B may have been smarter than students in Group A
B Group A may have studied more and practised more than Group B
C The experiment was not scientific and therefore the results cannot be used as sufficient evidence
D Students who did not eat almonds may be better in other activities

22

To make a working laptop, you need to have good coding skills and an excellent approach on hardware

Sam: "Sally is extremely good at coding. The only problem is that she does not know much about hardware. Regardless, she will make a working laptop."

Sally: "Sam has an excellent approach to hardware, however, he does not know much about coding and programming languages. He will certainly make one of the best working laptops."

If the information in the box is true, whose reasoning is correct?

A Neither Sam nor Sally
B Sally Only
C Both Sam and Sally
D Sam Only

23 Five houses stand together in a row. One person lives in each house; each person likes a different colour; they all have different gaming systems. We also know that:

- Andrew likes PlayStation and lives next to Danny, who is on the left end of the row and likes blue
- The person who lives in the middle likes green and plays the PC
- Ellie likes brown and lives at the end of the street on the right
- Carly lives one house away from Ellie
- Bruce likes to play the PC

Using the information above, who lives in the middle of the row?

A Andrew
B Bruce
C Danny
D Ellie

24 In history, primary sources are defined as firsthand evidence of an event that took place in the past. Examples of primary sources are diaries, correspondence, photographs, newspaper articles, and autobiographies – basically, anything that documents an event as it's happening, or a record of an event by someone who was there as a participant or observer.

Which one of the following conclusions is best supported by the passage above?

A Primary sources are directly from the event that took place, it is the most reliable source.
B Primary sources can be easy to find as long as you come from that time period.
C Primary sources are difficult to find in comparison to secondary sources.
D Primary sources are firsthand evidence that can be manufactured evidence to help sources work in the interests of the historian.

25 Recently there has been a movement of musicians who are demanding justice from the popular music-streaming service "Spotify". It has been called out for underpaying, misleading and exploiting artists and their music for financial gain. Artists have been arguing that Spotify's profit margins are so large for them to need 263 streams to earn $1.

Which of the following arguments below **weakens** the musician's rebellion?

A Artists work too hard on their discographies to be underpaid
B Just as everyone else, artists deserve to receive a living wage
C By increasing artist's pay Spotify would lose their large profit margins
D Streaming services do not own the music they provide and should pay artists more

26 The Hills Challenge is a competition in which four athletes compete against each other in four marathon races, run on consecutive days.

Points are awarded in each race, as follows:
first place 5 points
second place 3 points
third place 2 points
fourth place 1 point

This table shows the total points of the competitors in this year's Hills Challenge after each race.

name	Total points after race 1	Total points after race 2	Total points after race 3	Total points after race 4
Alice	5	6	7	9
Belinda	1	3	5	10
Charlie	2	7	10	11
Daniel	3	6	11	14

Who finished in a different position in each of the four races?

A Alice
B Belinda
C Charlie
D Daniel

27 A two-month study of major producers of ivory products showed that worldwide demand for elephant tusks for ivory had fallen sharply. Consequently, it is safe to assume that there will be a general decline in elephant poaching.

Which one of the following, if true, would most **weaken** the above argument?

A There are far fewer elephants than there were ten years ago, so poachers are finding it increasingly difficult to make a living from the ivory trade.
B Poachers now use high-powered rifles which make it far easier for them to kill larger numbers of elephants than was possible in the past.
C The worldwide demand for ivory fluctuates considerably at certain times of the year, so poachers stockpile ivory to sell when the market improves.
D More and more synthetic materials are being used as substitutes for ivory in the construction of such things as piano keys and billiard balls.

28 Jessica is making costumes for the 10 members of the Talent Dancers, for their annual show. The costumes can be made in a variety of colour combinations, as shown in the following table.

The table also shows the number of dancers who will have each variety of costume.

Costume colour	Number of dancers
100% red	3
100% blue	3
100% yellow	2
50% red, 50% blue	1
50% red, 50% yellow	1

Each costume can be made from exactly 2 m of material. The material comes in 10 m rolls and Jessica buys one roll in each of red, yellow, and blue.

How much red material will be left over?

A 5 m
B 4 m
C 3 m
D 2 m

29 At the beginning of this year, Vivian had $0 in her bank account.
The following graph shows the changes in the balance of money in her account last six months.

How many months did Vivian have more than $200 in her account?

A 1
B 2
C 3
D 4

30 Jesse wanted to figure out what was the most popular subject in his year level being: English, Maths, PE and Science. He did a survey of all the students at the school, and found the following:

- People who dislike PE also dislike Science.
- There are more people who enjoy Maths over English.
- Less people like Science over PE.
- More people enjoy English over PE.

Which was the most popular subject?

A English.
B Maths.
C PE.
D Science.

31 Erika's video stream is set to 720p to show a clear video, the higher the p the clearer the video.

Jiji: "I don't think your stream is at 720p right now since it is pixelated."

Erika: "No my stream is fine, it is on 480p right now."

If the information in the box is true, whose reasoning is correct?

A Jiji only.
B Erika only.
C Both Jiji and Erika.
D Neither Jiji nor Erika.

32 The smell of rain is linked to the feeling of cold and tends to smell musky. However, fire smells like ash, and is linked to the feeling of heat. The smell of grass is earthy and gives one the feeling of happiness. The smell of bread is fresh and provides a feeling of warmth.

If the above statements are correct, which of the following is **not** possible?

A Sitting around the campfire makes me feel hot.
B Standing in the bakery makes me feel warm due to the fresh smell of bread.
C Lying on the grass that smells like the ground makes me think of joyful memories.
D It is currently raining outside since it is musky and I feel warm.

33 The most common excuse for the poor performance of English school children in learning foreign languages is the fact that English is so widely spoken in the world. Thus, when the English travel to another country, they feel little need to become proficient in the local language. But that cannot explain why, amongst children who have never travelled outside their own country, the English are still out-performed by their overseas counterparts in foreign language acquisition. One is led to the inevitable conclusion that English schools are deficient in the teaching of languages.

Which of the following is the best statement of the **flaw** in this argument?

A It reaches its conclusion without considering other possible explanations for poor performance in languages.
B It overlooks the fact that other languages, for example, Spanish, are also widely spoken in the world.
C It is based upon evidence taken from an unrepresentative sample: those children who have not travelled abroad.
D It fails to offer any proof that the English are poor at learning foreign languages.

34

> At the video game competition, participants play a wakeboarding and cycling game. These two scores are then added together to give an overall score at the competition (for example, a participator with scores of 14 for wakeboarding and 2 for cycling will have an overall score of 16 in the competition).
>
> Pete and Melissa got the same overall score in the competition.

Pete: "If our scores for wakeboarding were different, then for cycling they must be different."

Melissa: "If our scores for cycling were the same, then for wakeboarding they must be different."

If the information in the box is true, whose reasoning is correct?

A Pete only.
B Both Pete and Melissa.
C Neither Pete nor Melissa.
D Melissa only.

35 This shows the number of books owned by a group of 125 students.

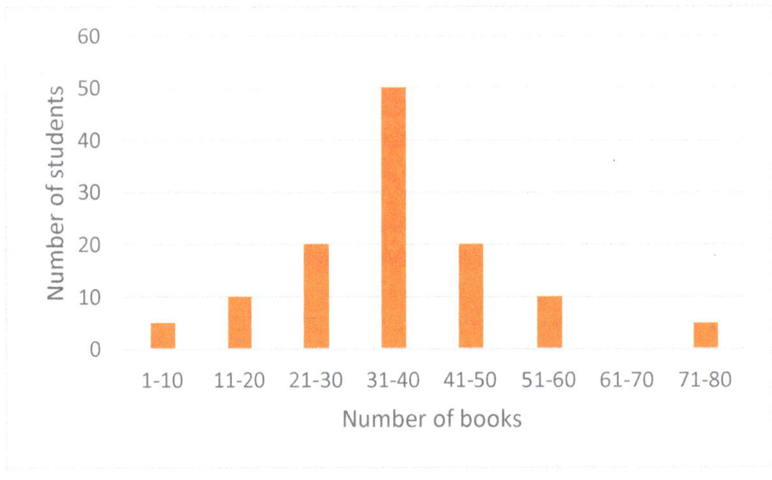

How many students do not own any books?

A 0
B 5
C 10
D 15

36 A train leaves Blacktown station at 10.50am. It stops at each station for 3 minutes at small stations for passengers to board and alight, and 6 minutes at major stations. It passes 6 small stations and 4 major stations throughout its route before ending at Central. Central and Blacktown are both major stations and are not included in the '4'. If it arrives at Central at 12.08pm, how long did the train spend travelling?

A 32 minutes
B 34 minutes
C 36 minutes
D 38 minutes

37 House prices have risen to far greater prices than ever before because of the extreme levels of borrowing money from banks. Due to these high prices, owning their own house has become hard for many people. Those who can 'own' their own home normally have lots of debt that needs to be repaid. Since the recent financial crisis is part of the reason why many people could not pay back their debts, governments should try to tackle the problem at its root and take action to prevent even more increases in house prices.

Which of the following, if true, will best **strengthen** the above argument?

A House prices begin to fall by themselves after a few years have passed
B People tend to buy houses more than rent, since they think that is better in the long run
C There is not much the government can do to stop house prices from rising
D The gap between the average salary of the individual and the average house price has been widening over the past few years

38

> The main reason private schools are so popular is that they are extremely good at getting their students into elite universities. Only 7% of students attend private schools but they account for 40% of students at Oxford University and Cambridge University. Since entry to the top universities is dependent on exam results, private school students must be achieving higher grades than those in public schools. Higher grades are the result of good teaching, so the teaching methods in private schools must be better than the teaching methods in public schools.

Which of the following statements, if true, most **weakens** the above argument?

A Public schools often have more options for classes, after-school activities, and varied curriculums than private schools.
B Better teachers tend to work at private schools because they receive a higher pay compared to the pay teachers receive in public schools
C Elite universities also consider schools with good reputations
D Private schools have higher standards for students, starting from the year they enter the school

39 The world has been struck with a virus, thus everyone has to stay inside to ensure the virus doesn't spread any further. Since everyone is staying in their homes, they are no people going shopping in shopping centers. Due to this, shops are not earning enough money, so they cannot pay for the rent to stay in that store.

Which one of the following is an assumption made in the passage above?

A The virus will not last for long
B People will never buy from affected shops again, even after the pandemic is over
C The shops only have physical stores and do not have any online websites that can earn more money
D No one is listening to the rules and are leaving homes despite the warnings

40 The government has apologized for the mistreatment of people with coloured skin in the past. This is an improvement that will help the community grow. However, the apology for the historical injustice was long overdue.

Which one of these statements is the best conclusion to the above argument?

A The historical injustice should have been apologized for a very long time ago
B The community is not learning from their past mistakes
C The government should not have to apologise for others' mistakes
D It is the responsibility of the government to ensure that this injustice does not occur again

Selective Practice Test Paper
Thinking Skills 9 (Time allowed: 40 min)

INSTRUCTIONS

1 Write your Name on the cover page.

2 There are 40 questions in this paper. For each question there are four possible answers, A, B, C and D. Choose the one correct answer and record your choice on the separate answer sheet. If you make a mistake, erase thoroughly and try again.

3 You will not lose marks for incorrect answers, so you should attempt all 40 questions

4 You must complete the answer sheet within the time limit. There will not be any extra time at the end of the exam to record your answers on the answer sheet.

5 You can use the question paper for working out, but no extra paper is allowed.

Name: ____

1 The following graph shows the number of books borrowed at a library per day.

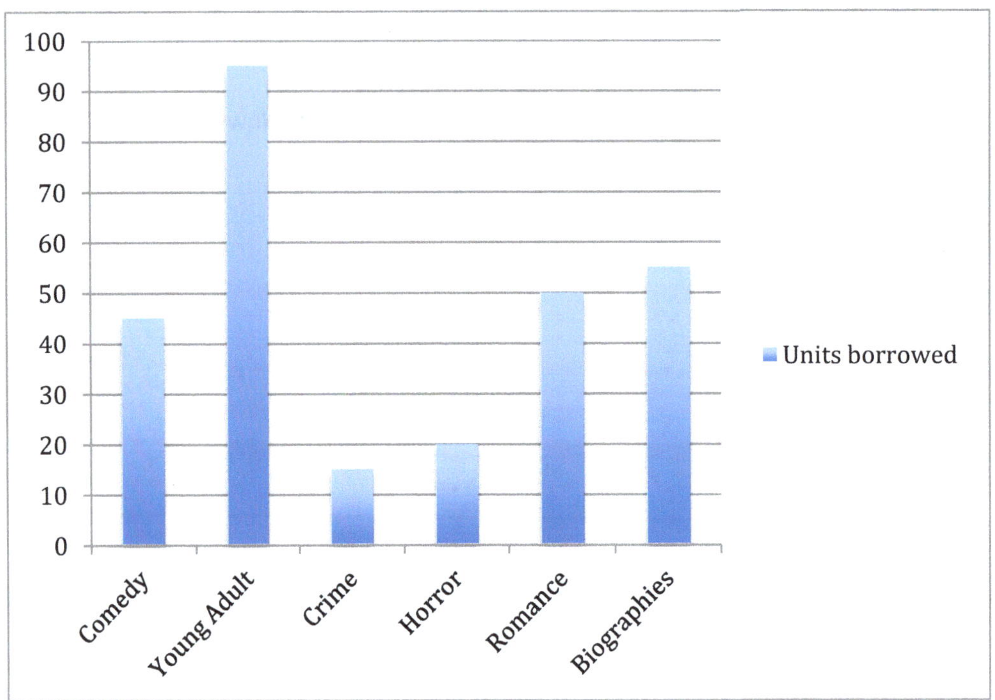

The library is open from 9am to 5pm. What is the average number of books borrowed per hour?

A 30
B 25
C 40
D 35

2 Research has shown that people need to eat a balanced diet, including all food groups, which eventually leads to a much healthier lifestyle. However, most American citizen's diets are made up of fast food and unhealthy snacks. We need to spend more money on education programs to get people to realise that they need a healthier diet and lifestyle.

Which one of these statements is an assumption that the argument makes?

A American citizens do not eat healthy foods because of the influence of their friends and families
B American people may still not adopt a healthy lifestyle even if they learn more about their bodies and the effects of foods
C American citizens do not care about a healthy diet and lifestyle
D Most people in America do not have a balanced diet due to their lack of education

3 A research paper showed that the demand for turtle shell jewellery has fallen sharply. Consequently, it is safe to assume that there will be a general decline in turtle poaching.

Which of the following, if true, would most **weaken** the above argument?

A Poachers only think to poach animals for the sake of earning money
B Many people have already bought many pieces of turtle shell jewelry, thus they do not need to buy anymore
C Turtle shell jewelry has gone out of fashion in recent years
D People do not only poach turtles for their shells. They also poach them for their eggs, meat and skin

4 In the following pair of images, the right-hand image is the result of applying a series of changes to the left-hand image. These changes are a difference in the order of the shapes and the application of rotations to two of the shapes:

Which one of the following pairs of images shows the same series of changes applied to the left-hand image to produce the right-hand image?

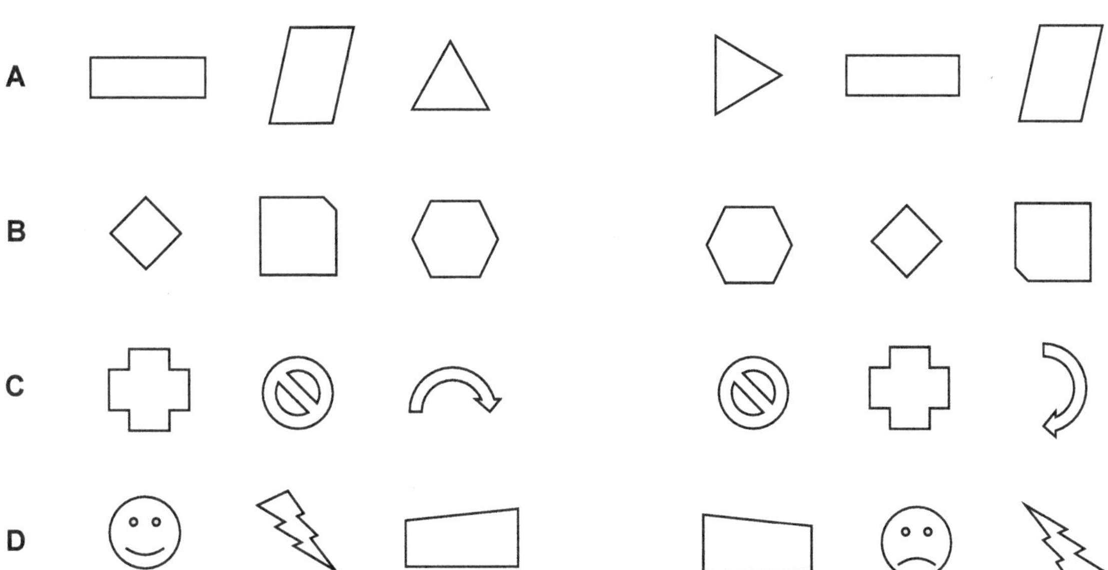

5

> Four friends were playing a game together at a party.
>
> - Sarah beat Chloe but did not collect as many coins as Chloe
> - Meg lost to Sarah and did not collect as many coins as Sarah
> - Rebecca placed first but did not collect as many coins as Meg

If the information in the box is true, which of the following statements **cannot** be true?

A Chloe collected the most amount of coins
B Meg could have come last or second last
C Meg collected the least number of coins
D Sarah came second in the race and collected the second-highest number of coins

6 There were 4 competitors in the school's Victor Ludorum competition to select the best athlete. Competitors competed in up to 4 events. The scoring was 5 points for the winner down to 1 point for the 5th place. At the end of the competition, a contestant's worst event was ignored and the sum of the points for the best three events was calculated. The winner was the highest scorer.

The table below shows the finishing places in the four events:

	High jump	100m	1500m	Long jump
Adam	4	2	1	4
Belinda	2	4	2	1
Chris	1	1	4	2
Dianne	3	3	3	3

Who won?

A Adam
B Belinda
C Chris
D Dianne

7 What would the cross-section of the figure below look like?

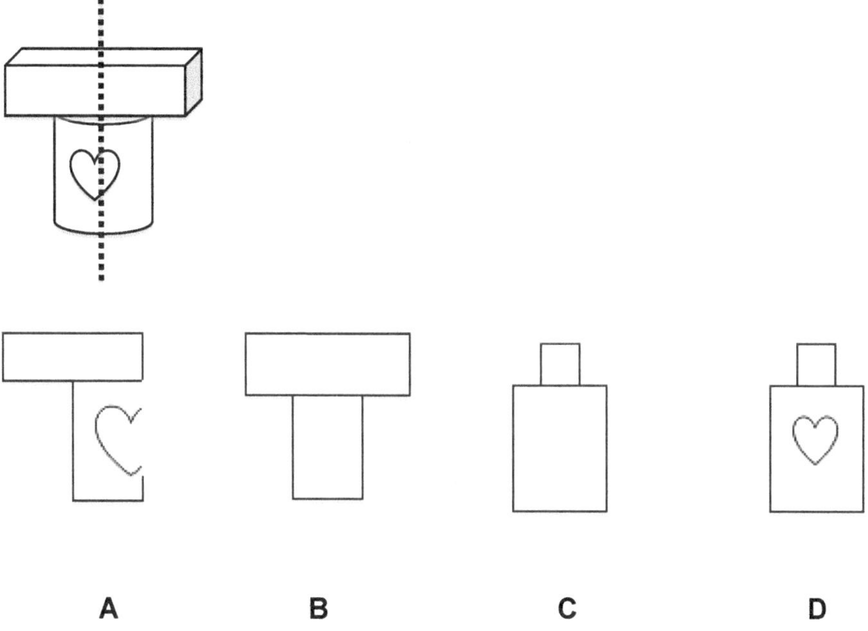

8 **Principal**: "We believe that these students are having academic problems because they spend too much time on school sports and too little time studying. Therefore, I am prohibiting all students who are having academic problems from taking part in sports. This will ensure that these students spend more time studying."

Which one of these statements shows the mistake that the Principal has made?

A They have assumed that more time studying may lead to better academics
B They have not researched the problem enough before making the decision
C They have ignored the potential influence that ordinary students may have on these academically-troubled students
D Principal has ignored the benefits that sport may have on academics

9

The results of a colour survey are as follows:

- Everyone who said they liked pink also liked purple
- Everyone who liked blue also liked yellow
- Everyone who liked yellow disliked orange
- Everyone who liked purple liked blue

If Tessa participated in the survey, which of the following statements is true?

A Tessa likes purple so she also must like pink
B Tessa likes purple so she must dislike orange
C Tessa likes blue so she also must like pink
D Tessa likes orange so she also must like blue

10 Which figure will complete this sequence?

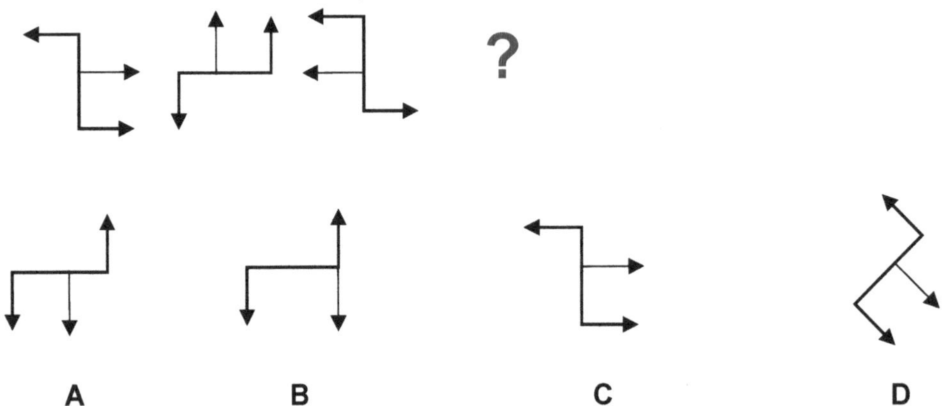

11

> It is impossible for the pressing machine to start without the sinking machine operating beforehand.

1. Since the sinking machine is operating, the pressing machine may be started
2. Since the pressing machine is currently operating, the sinking machine must have already stopped

If the information in the box is true, which reasoning is correct?

A 1 only
B 2 only
C Both 1 and 2
D Neither 1 nor 2

12 Henry is brainstorming present ideas for his grandma.

He knows that:
His grandma likes to knit and crochet in her spare time.
She spends her Sundays every week with grandpa at the golf club.
Her favourite gifts have been things that she needs for her hobbies.

If this is true, what present would his grandma **most** enjoy?

A A golf club
B A ball of yarn
C Knitting lessons
D A wooly sweater

13 This shape is reflected to the left.

Which shape below shows the correct reflection to the left?

A **B** **C** **D**

14 No pork are chicken breasts. Some meats are pork. Therefore, some meats are not chicken breasts.

Which of the following most closely parallels the reasoning in the above argument?

A No sour worms are lollies. No lollies are chocolates. Therefore, no sour worms are chocolates.
B No dodgeballs are basketballs. Some balls are dodgeballs. Therefore, some balls are not basketballs.
C Some beef are steaks. All steaks are meat. Therefore, some beef is meat
D No crickets are bugs. Some flies are bugs. Therefore, some crickets are flies

15 Chris and Daniel want to use a code to send secret messages to each other. In the code, each letter of the alphabet is represented by a one-digit number, as follows:

A	B	C	D	E	F	G	H	I	J	K	L	M	N	O	P	Q	R	S	T	U	V	W	X	Y	Z
1	2	3	4	5	6	7	8	9	0	1	2	3	4	5	6	7	8	9	0	1	2	3	4	5	6

For example, the word LINE would be written in the code as 2-9-4-5.

To test the system, Chris writes four words in the code and sends them to Daniel. Daniel tries to decode them, and gets the following answers:

BEEN

FIND

MAKE

DOWN

Daniel is confident that he has three of these words correctly, but he is unsure about the other one.

Which word is Daniel unsure about?

A BEEN
B FIND
C MAKE
D DOWN

16 Soccer practice occurs every night but Vince can only go every 4th night. Victor can go every 3rd night. Today is Saturday both Vince and Victor are attending. What day will it be the next time Victor and Vince see each other at training?

A Tuesday
B Wednesday
C Thursday
D Friday

17 Australia is considering a new law system, where if a crime was motivated by a sincere desire to achieve some larger good, then the punishment for the crime may be decreased, even for the worst crimes.

Poppy: This system means that people will have no punishment for stealing food from grocery stores if they are too poor to afford it.

Rosie: This system can be biased, since motives are subjective and can be thought of differently by different people.

If the information in the box is true, whose reasoning is correct?

A Poppy
B Rosie
C Both Poppy and Rosie
D Neither Poppy nor Rosie

18 Karen left her house to go shopping at a faraway outlet. A little while after she left, she had a feeling that she had left the stove gas on. She decided to go back and check whether or not the gas was still on.

Which of the following best describes the principle underlying the above argument?

A Always listen to your parents
B You should never stop at a faraway outlet
C Never listen to your gut feeling because it is a waste of time
D Better safe than sorry

19 This 3D shape was originally a rectangular prism. What is the minimal number of blocks that have been removed from the cube leaving this solid?

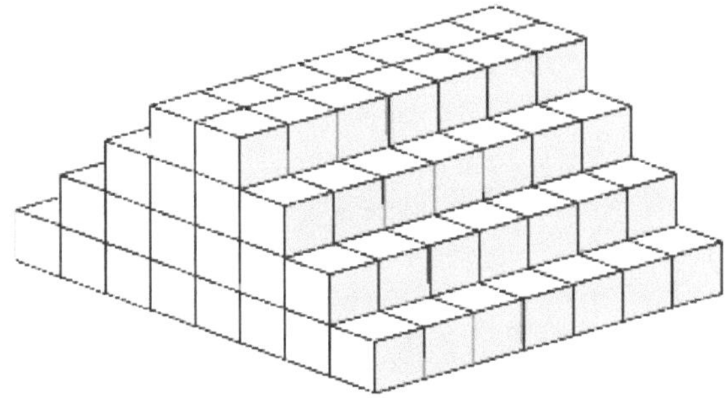

A 64
B 72
C 78
D 84

20 Charlie's class wanted to find out how a person's intelligence is affected by what genre of books a person reads. They asked 3 people to take a quick test, who said they read romance fiction, science fiction and action books respectively. These were the results of the test:

- The person who reads romance fiction scored higher than the person who reads action books
- The person who reads romance fiction did not receive the highest score

What did the person who reads science fiction place?

A First
B Second
C Third
D Tied for first

21

> Even in ancient times, specialist farms existed only in dense, urban cities. These farms grew only a single type of crop or livestock.

Mandy: Kadshim was probably a largely uninhabited ceremonial structure rather than a dense, urban city, since the land in Kadshim could never have supported any farms except mixed farms, which grow multiple types of crops of livestock.

Which one of the following sentences shows the mistake that Mandy has made?

A She assumes that ceremonial structures cannot support specialised farms
B She takes an ambiguous and broad notion about specialised farms and applies it to a specific city
C Although specialised farms only existed where there were urban cities, that does not mean that urban cities must have specialised farms.
D The conclusion is simply a restatement of one of the initial arguments

22 These are three different views of the same cube.

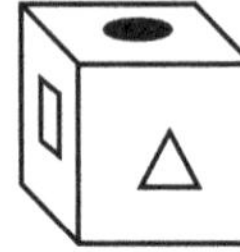 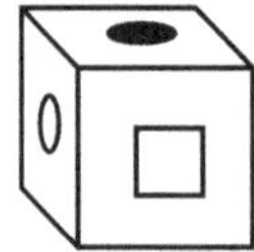 

The triangle is opposite the face with:

A 
B
C 
D

23

> If children are sitting in rows in a classroom, the teacher can have eye contact with all of them while they are explaining something to them. This is not always possible if they are sitting in groups around tables. Also, when they look up, instead of seeing the child opposite in a group and being tempted to talk, they see the teacher. So, sitting in rows helps children to concentrate better on their work and should therefore be the standard arrangement in every school classroom.

Which one of the following, if true, would most **weaken** the above argument?

A Some children are easily distracted no matter which formation they sit in
B Research has shown that classes with their tables set in rows have done better in exams than those with tables in group formations
C When students sit in rows, everyone can see what is being taught on the whiteboard
D Students cannot learn well with their back facing the teacher

24 These 9 congruent squares can be rearranged into a square with an area of 225 cm^2

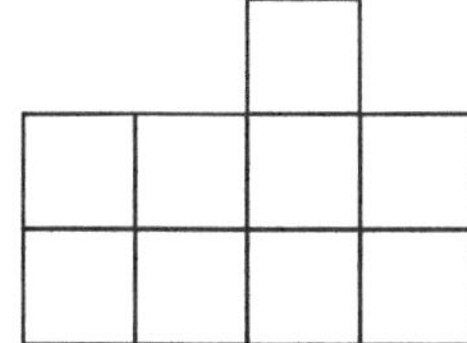

What is the perimeter of this shape?

A 66 cm
B 70 cm
C 72 cm
D 75 cm

25 Using the information and your answer for Question 24 above, which of these shapes made of congruent squares have a perimeter of 100 cm?

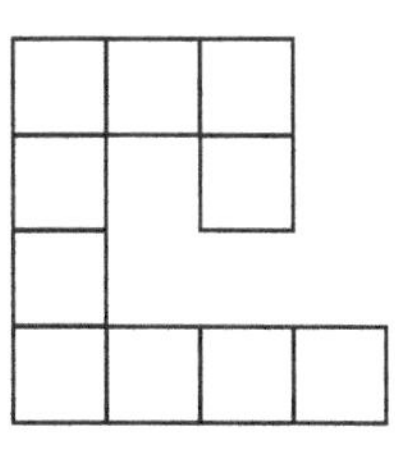
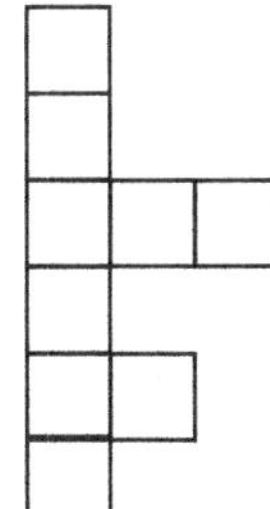
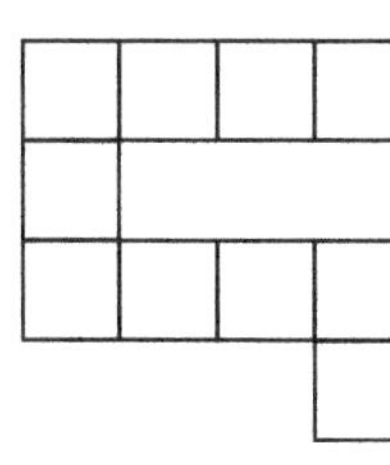
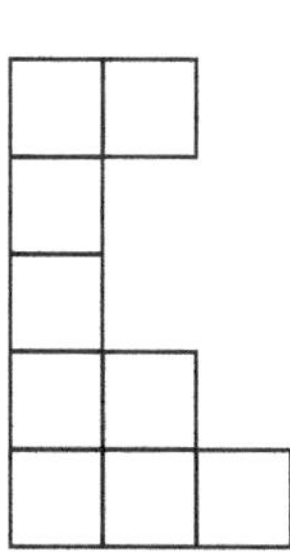

A **B** **C** **D**

26 Charlie is trying to start a successful business. He starts by doing every task in front of him in detail. Soon, he worked his way up to become a very successful businessman.

Which one of these statements best describes the principle underlying the above argument?

A Businesses are hard to build especially if everything is done in detail
B Every large goal is achieved through taking small steps and working your way up to that goal
C Always trust yourself to do the right thing and make the right decisions
D There is no guarantee that you will succeed and when you try something, but it is always worth the try

27

> According to a recent survey, people believe that about a quarter of the population will become victims of a violent crime in the next year, whereas crime statistics show that it is only about 1%. Furthermore, those with the greatest fear of crime are the least likely to be affected. The elderly is the most fearful, although victims are most likely to be young males. Over the last few years, there has been an increase in the number of television shows which show crimes. These shows add to people's fears by making it look more common than it is. It is time that we stopped making such shows.

Which of the following, if true, would most **strengthen** the above argument?

A Some types of violent crime have declined over the past couple of years
B People who produce the shows do not do much research on the crimes
C Older people's fears of violent crimes are increased after watching the TV shows
D The survey was taken to help update the crime statistics

28 Any railway customer who has to wait for a train that is delayed by more than 20 minutes is entitled to a refund of $5. Anyone who has to wait for a train that is delayed by more than 10 minutes but less than 20 minutes is entitled to a refund of $3.

The table below shows the scheduled arrival time and the actual arrival time for 5 customers' trains.

customer	Scheduled arrival time	Actual arrival time
1	08:20	08:35
2	10:17	10:40
3	11:45	12:00
4	15:50	15:55
5	20:30	20:55

All of the customers who were entitled to a refund did receive the refund from the railway company.

How much money did the railway company have to pay out in total to these customers?

A $24
B $21
C $19
D $16

29 People with high blood pressure are generally more nervous and anxious than people who do not have high blood pressure.

Jane: "My brother has a 'hypertensive' personality, so he is often easily scared and always gets nervous before going to work. He must have high blood pressure.

Which of the following sentences shows the mistake that Jane has made?

A High blood pressure does not always mean that the person is more nervous and anxious
B People with a 'hypertensive' personality may eventually grow out of it
C A 'hypertensive' personality does not mean that Jane's brother always gets nervous before going to work
D Just because high blood pressure causes specific traits, that does not prove that people with those traits always have high blood pressure

30 7 Plots of land within a community garden are allocated for people to grow fruit and vegetables. The plots come in a variety of sizes. The garden consists of seven plots as described in the table below.

	Length (metres)	Width (metres)
Plot 1	4	1
Plot 2	4	4
Plot 3	5	5
Plot 4	3	1
Plot 5	6	4
Plot 6	3	3
Plot 7	10	4

Which one of the plans below could show the plots in the garden? (For each plot the length is the longest side and the width is the shortest side.)

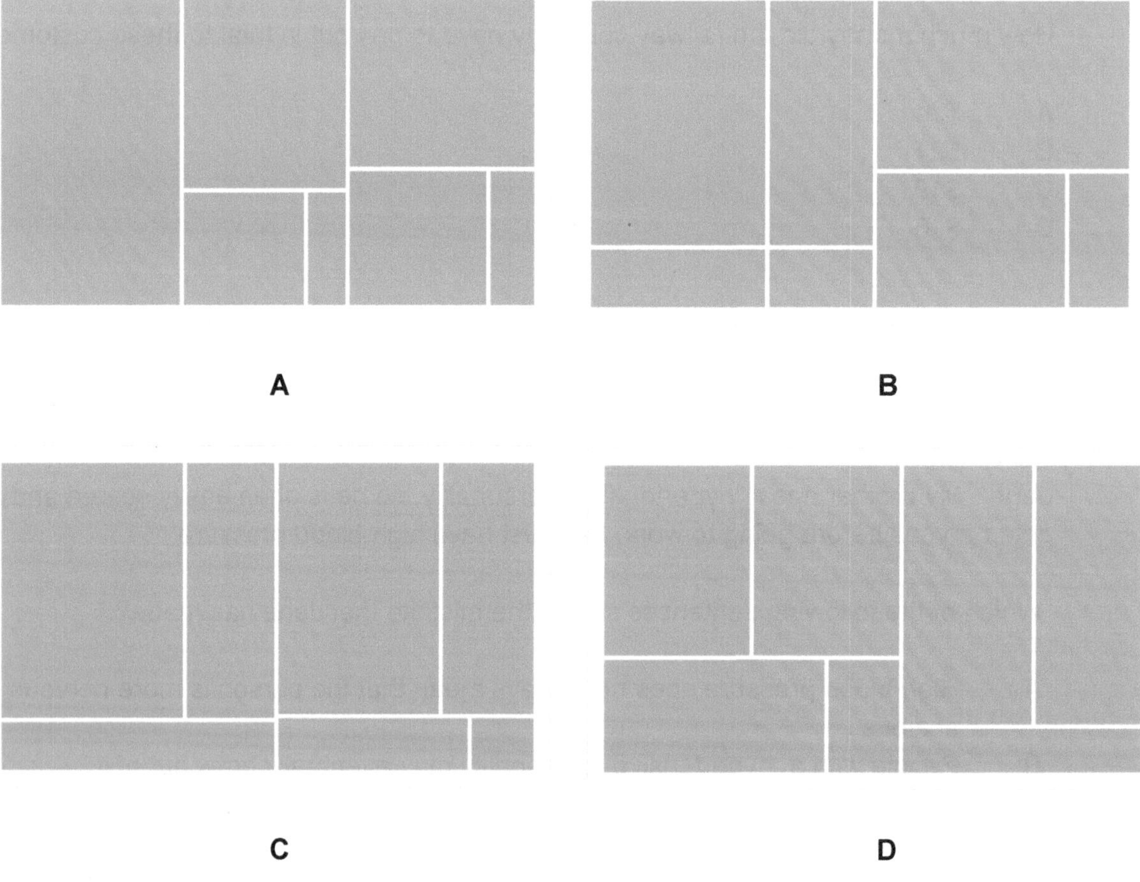

31

Two kinds of tree are most popular in the Jeriko Rainforest, the Oak tree and Maple tree. Kaitlin and Bob are investigating the population of each kind of tree.

Bob: "We have searched nearly the entire forest and found 2000 Oak trees and 5400 Maple Trees."

Kaitlin: "Wow, seems like there needs to be more Oak Trees"

Which one of the following sentences shows the mistake Kaitlin has made?

A A parasite may have infected Oak trees, reducing their numbers.
B The Oak tree could be more populous in other locations.
C The Maple Tree is more suited to the rainforest condition.
D Other tree species may not have been accounted for.

32 "Happiness is based on a just discrimination of what is necessary, then of what is not necessary or destructive and lastly of what is destructive."

If this is true, which of these sentences must also be true?

A If there is discrimination of what not necessary or destructive then there is no happiness.
B If there has been discrimination of what is destructive then there was no discrimination of what is necessary.
C If there is no discrimination for what was not destructive or necessary then there is no discrimination.
D If there is no discrimination of what is not necessary then there is happiness.

33 The Wakanda Census Bureau published the following table showing the number and percentage of people in poverty by geographic region in 2021.

Region	All	East	West	South	North
Number of people (thousands)	37000	8500	15000	7500	6000
Percentage of region population	14	13	15	10	20

Which one of the following charts could represent all of the percentages shown in the table?

34 Four Electronic Companies - GE Electrics, Mango, Watt and Boom, sell monitors. Maverick needs to get a monitor that is not too expensive but still offers quality images and video.

Boom offers better quality than GE Electrics, but less than Mango. GE Electrics is more expensive than Watt. Boom costs more than Watt, but is cheaper than Mango.

Which of the four Electronic Companies will Maverick choose?

A GE Electrics
B Mango
C Boom
D Watt

35 A group of kids was surveyed on what their favourite toys to play with were. It was found that whoever liked playing with dolls liked playing with teddy bears. Whoever liked playing with teddy bears liked playing with action figures. Whoever liked playing with action figures liked playing with toy cars.

Ben participated in the survey. Which of the following statements is **not** true?

A Ben liked playing with action figures because he liked playing with dolls
B Ben liked playing with toy cars because he liked playing with teddy bears
C Ben liked playing with toy cars because he liked playing with action figures
D Ben liked playing with dolls because he liked playing with action figures

36 "Recent accidents in the oil industry have made safety a very important public issue that must be discussed."

Citizen: "Because the oil industry cannot be expected to behave itself, the government must step in and take action to solve this issue."

Which of the following statements shows the mistake made by the citizen?

A They do not discuss the safety issues in detail
B They assume that the government has people working in the oil industry
C They have not considered other options to solve the safety issue
D The oil industry has always had safety issues, but has never needed the government to step in

37 Which of the following has the largest capacity?

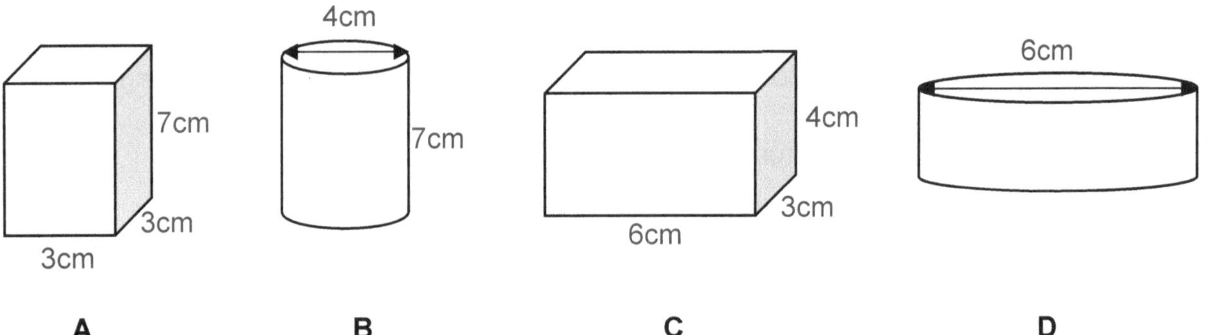

38 A Christmas bonus is being offered to the employee who secures the most number of sales across the next 20-day working period.
The Christmas bonus will be an additional 20% of an employee's wages. The company are using this new incentive as a way of boosting sales during their peak time. The Managing Director says that this bonus incentive will continue each year, if it proves to be successful.
The table below shows the top four employees' sales results recorded weekly (5 working days).

Name	Dennis	Andrew	Vivian	Jessica
Week 1	3	9	1	5
Week 2	3	2	4	5
Week 3	6	0	7	3
Week 4	9	9	8	7

Which employee will receive the Christmas bonus?

A Dennis
B Andrew
C Vivian
D Jessica

39 Alexa wants to figure out how different songs affect the mood of people at a party by playing various songs throughout the party. This is what they found:

- Less people got up to dance to R&B than Hip-Hop.
- More people got up to R&B than to Blues.
- More people danced to Pop than Hip-Hop.

Which of the following can be concluded from the information above?

A The least popular song people danced to was Blues.
B The majority of people danced to Hip-Hop.
C Hip-Hop and Blues were generally more popular to be danced to.
D The least popular songs to dance to were R&B and Pop.

40 Peter wants to photocopy a newsletter for his local chess club. He needs at least 60 copies. The newsletter has 2 sides, and will be printed in black and white, double sided. The prices for his local print shop are shown below.

		Black and White	Colour
Photocopying	1 – 24	5¢ per side	50¢ per side
	25 – 49	3¢ per side	30¢ per side
	50 – 149	2¢ per side	20¢ per side
	150 over	1¢ per side	10¢ per side

What is the price he will have to pay?

A $2.00
B $2.40
C $2.80
D $3.20

Selective Practice Test Paper

Thinking Skills 10 (Time allowed: 40 min)

INSTRUCTIONS

1 Write your Name on the cover page.

2 There are 40 questions in this paper. For each question there are four possible answers, A, B, C and D. Choose the one correct answer and record your choice on the separate answer sheet. If you make a mistake, erase thoroughly and try again.

3 You will not lose marks for incorrect answers, so you should attempt all 40 questions

4 You must complete the answer sheet within the time limit. There will not be any extra time at the end of the exam to record your answers on the answer sheet.

5 You can use the question paper for working out, but no extra paper is allowed.

Name: ______________________________

1 A paper square has been folded into quarters and shapes are cut and put.

When opened it looks like this.

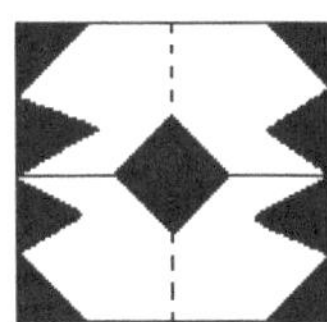

Choose the folded paper which shows how the paper was cut.

A

B

C

D

2 A computer system codes and decodes numbers using the alphabet.

For example, BCE represents the number 30 and YB represents the number 50.

What letters are possible codes for the number 144?

A CJ
B HR
C ZM
D AFK

3 Two of the same shape would cover the shaded area of this rectangle.

Choose the shape.

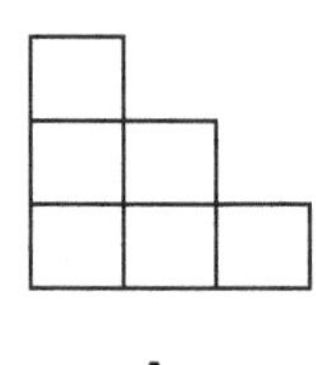

A

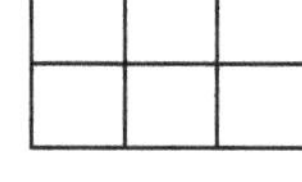

B

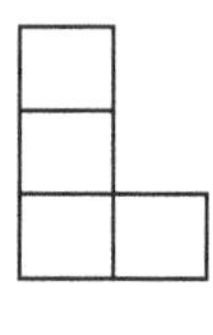

C

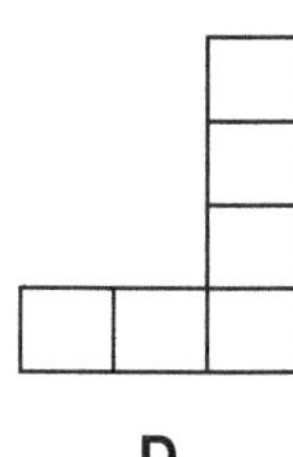

D

4 In order to be able to feed the world's growing population, we need ever more food, which must be diverse, balanced and of good quality to ensure the progress and well-being of humankind. Bees are renowned for their role in providing high-quality food (honey, royal jelly and pollen) and other products used in healthcare and other sectors (beeswax, propolis, honeybee venom). But the work of bees entails much more!

Which of the following, if true, most **strengthens** the argument above?

A Bees pollinate three-fourths of the plants that humans need for consumption.
B They pollinate flowers the most which contributes to the decreasing number of flowers.
C Bees that sting die after doing so since they lose their tails.
D There has been a wide variety of bees that are not easy to harvest honey from.

5 Zack does not like to drink water because he prefers to drink coca cola. Since drinking water is essential for staying hydrated and maintaining a healthy lifestyle, Zack must not be healthy.

Which of the following most closely matches this argument in structure?

A Billy does not like to exercise. Since exercise makes you healthier, she must not be healthy
B Billy is not healthy because she does not like to exercise, as exercise makes you healthy
C Running on the treadmill is not needed to become healthier. Billy does not run on the treadmill. Therefore, she is not healthy
D Billy does not enjoy exercising because it is hard. Since exercise makes you healthier, she must not be healthy.

6 Marie wanted to know the most popular piece of clothing being bought at her shop from t-shirts, jackets, jeans or skirts. She did a survey over the week and found the following:

- The number of people who like jeans is 35.
- The number of people who like skirts is 9 x 2.
- More than 100 people like t-shirts.
- The number of people who like jeans and jackets is 70.
- 200 people were surveyed.

How many people like t-shirts?

A 110.
B 111.
C 112.
D 113.

7 At that moment he had a thought that he'd never imagine he'd consider. "I could just cheat," he thought, "and that would solve the problem." He tried to move on from the thought but it was persistent. It didn't want to go away and, if he was honest with himself, he didn't want it to.

Which one of these statements based on the passage is true for Bob's situation?

A Cheating will get Bob in trouble with his parents.
B That cheating is immoral.
C If Bob cheats his problem will be solved but he won't learn from it.
D Bob can't stop thinking about cheating.

8 Many women who aspire to participate and win in these beauty pageants starve themselves every day to become thin and look pretty like their ideals who won the beauty contest. The development of eating disorders like bulimia has become very common.

Which one of these statements, if true, most **weakens** the argument above?

A These contests set unrealistic beauty standards for women and often promote stereotypes.
B These contests have eligibility restrictions on age, marriage and pregnancy which can discriminate against many.
C Beauty pageants have become more inclusive and have created a platform where women can express issues they are passionate about
D Many even become a victim of body shaming that also leads to poor mental health just because of these irrational quests to idolize a certain body type

9

> The Northern Intercity Railway employs ticket inspectors to check that everyone travelling on a train has a valid ticket, and catch anyone trying to ride for free. Anyone caught without a ticket has to pay a $500 fine. In the last five years, not a single person has been caught without a valid ticket.

Linda: "If I go onto the train today without a valid ticket, I will not be caught since no one else has either"

Which one of the following shows the mistake Linda has made?

A The ticket inspectors are easy to get past.
B Linda can only get caught if she turns herself in.
C Linda can still get caught regardless of whether others are caught or not.
D Linda will be the first to get caught ever.

10 To play a football pools game, participants must select four matches from the fifty on the coupon. Points are scored depending on the result of each match as follows:

If the home team wins, the participant scores 1.0 point
If the away team wins, the participant scores 1.5 points
If the match is a draw, the participant scores 3.0 points

Which of the following total scores for the four matches is **not** possible?

A 8.5 points
B 9.0 points
C 9.5 points
D 10.0 points

11

> Due to crowd restrictions, the Drone Show can only be seen from two places: The harbour or the Milsons Lookout. Milsons Lookout has been impossible to access due to the flooding and immense rain the past two weeks.

Harry: "The Drone Show looked incredible!! I saw it about three weeks ago, don't remember where but it must have been at Milsons Lookout"

Chloe: "My family and I saw it yesterday. My brother took an amazing photo of the display from the harbour"

If the information in the box is true, whose reasoning is correct?

A Neither Harry nor Chloe
B Both Harry and Chloe
C Harry only
D Chloe only

12 Five houses stand together in a row. One person lives in each house; each person likes a different device and drink. We also know that:

- Louis likes to use a laptop and lives at the end on the right
- Teddy lives two houses from Louis and likes to drink Pepsi
- Niall lives in between the person that likes to drink Pepsi and the person that likes to drink orange juice
- Corrina lives on the right of Jimmy and uses an iPhone

Using the information above, who likes to drink orange juice?

A Louis
B Niall
C Teddy
D Corinna

13 All trees have leaves. An oak is a tree. Therefore oaks have leaves.

Which one of the following most closely parallels the reasoning used in the argument?

A All leaves grow on trees. That plant has leaves. Therefore that plant is a tree.
B All oaks have leaves. That tree has leaves. Therefore that tree is an oak.
C All plants have leaves. That leaf is an oak leaf. Therefore all plants are oaks.
D All trees have leaves. That plant has leaves. Therefore that plant is a tree.

14 Jars of Bespoke coffee weighing 200g are normally $5.00 at Coles and Woolworth, but both supermarkets have a special offer this week:

Coles	Woolworth
Bespoke coffee	Bespoke coffee
200g off per kg	40% off

By how much per kilogram is Woolworth's offer better value for money than Coles's?

A $2.50 per kg
B $5.00 per kg
C $7.00 per kg
D $7.50 per kg

15 There are some benefits of playing video games. In shooting games, the character may be running and shooting at the same time. This requires the real-world player to keep track of the position of the character, where he/she is heading, his speed, where the gun is aiming, if the gunfire is hitting the enemy, and so on.

Which one of these statements, if true, most **strengthens** the argument above?

- **A** Children who play more violent video games are more likely to have increased aggressive thoughts, feelings, and behaviours
- **B** Video games can train their brains to come up with creative ways to solve puzzles and other problems in short bursts
- **C** Video games can be addictive for kids, and kids' addiction to video games increases their depression and anxiety levels
- **D** Children may spend less time in other activities such as doing homework, reading, sports, and interacting with family and friends

16 From point T, I moved:

- 10 metres north
- 20 metres west
- 10 metres south
- 30 metres west
- 20 metres south
- 30 metres east

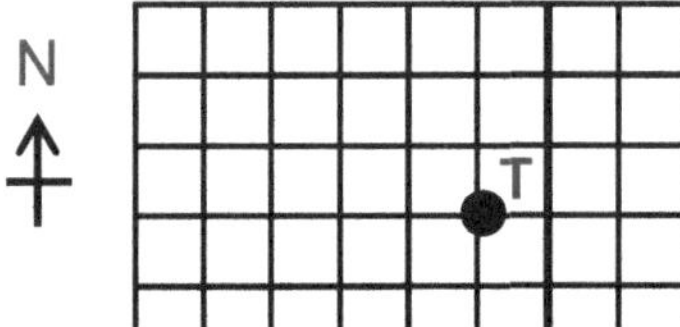

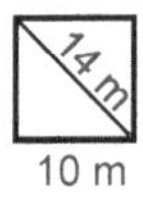

How far, and in which direction am I from T now?

- **A** 28m south west
- **B** 40m north east
- **C** 28m north east
- **D** 40m south west

17 Paul's school was choosing people to join the Relay team. To be considered, the coach looked at last year's top runners, the end of year school report and the first semester grades.

If a student had come in the top 5 in the last Athletics carnival, they only need to do well in their first semester grades. If they did not then they must do well in both their first semester grades and end of year school report or do extremely well in their end of year school report.

Paul came second last year in the School Athletics carnival but did not make it in. What must have been the reason for this?

- **A** He did badly in his first semester grades
- **B** He did badly at the end of the year school report
- **C** He did badly in both his first semester grades and the end of year report
- **D** He only did well in his first semester grades

18 Sharks have a reputation for being incredibly dangerous. However, within the past fifty years, less than 500 fatal shark attacks have been recorded worldwide. While this might seem like a lot, let's consider that more people die at the hands of other people, from preventable diseases, and poor lifestyles.

Which of the following is the best conclusion for the above argument?

A We need to find ways to prevent shark attacks.
B Sharks are less dangerous than people.
C We should demonise poor lifestyles and other people more than sharks.
D Sharks do not deserve to be demonised as much as they are.

19 Which of the following is **not** a possible view of the structure when it is rotated in any way?

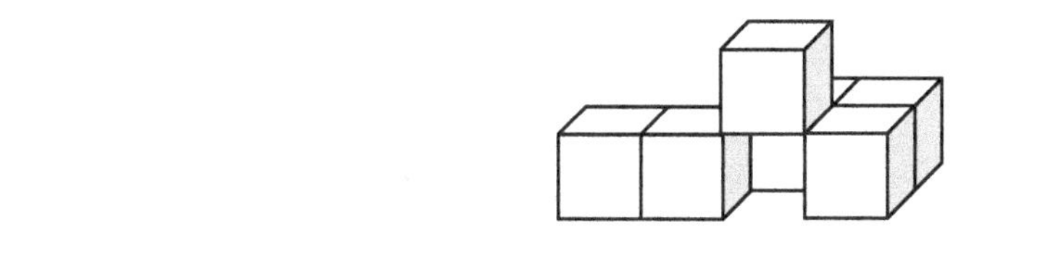

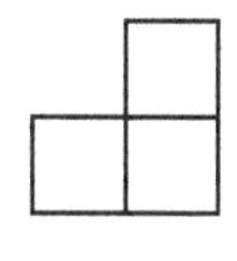

A

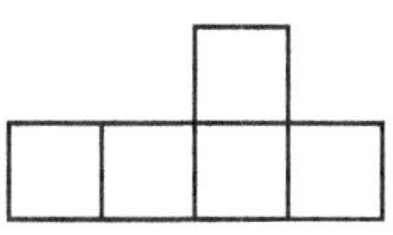

B

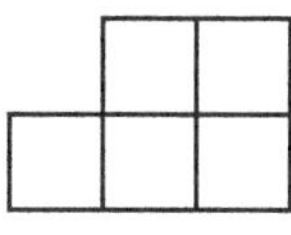

C

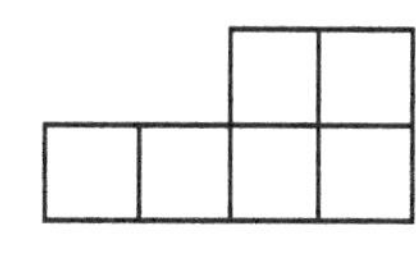

D

20 Ms Hong's class is reviewing a movie together. The following table shows how many students gave a particular score out of 5 for the movie.

Score	1	2	3	4	5
Number of students	3	1	9	5	2

What was the average score given by Ms Hong's class?

A 3.1
B 3.7
C 4.0
D 4.5

21 Below shows the earnings across different departments in a company. The earnings are recorded for different years.

Work out the total earnings from the department of finance.

A 220,150
B 218,540
C 221,000
D 215,750

22 There are two parts to your journey: for the first part, you travel 63 kilometres at a constant speed of 70 km/h. You arrive at the service station at 11:00am. You stay there for 30 minutes. You finish the second part of your journey at 1:00pm, travelling a total of 150 kilometres.

How long does the first part of your journey take?

A 36 minutes
B 54 minutes
C 1 hour 8 minutes
D 1 hour 10 minutes

23 Body piercings have become a staple in modern society. Many people have their ears, nose, eyebrows, and lips pierced. However, society still deems body piercings as unprofessional, meaning that many are rejected from job interviews simply because they might have a 'bad image'. This is nothing more than discrimination.

Which of the following, if true, would **weaken** the above argument?

A Society already has changed to become less judgemental towards people with body piercings.
B There are anti-discrimination laws to prevent such behaviour.
C Many jobs are customer-facing, which means that image needs to be taken into account during a job interview.
D This would not happen if people did not wear body piercings.

24 To pass the time on a long car journey, two children were playing a counting game.

Julia counted the number of animals they saw, and Tim counted their legs.

After 15 minutes, all they had seen were birds and sheep. Julia had counted 13 animals and Tim had counted 36 legs.

How many sheep had they seen?

A 4
B 5
C 6
D 8

25 In a survey of 1000 people, everyone that likes lollies likes chocolate. Everyone that liked chocolate liked sour candy but no one who liked sour candy liked licorice.

Kenny, Tim, Jessica and Alex all took part in the survey.

Based on the above information, which one of the following must be true?

A If Alex likes lollies, he also likes licorice.
B If Jessica does not like lollies, she does not like chocolate.
C If Tim does not like chocolate, he does not like sour candy.
D If Kenny likes chocolate, he does not like licorice.

26 Choose the two shapes that join to form a square.

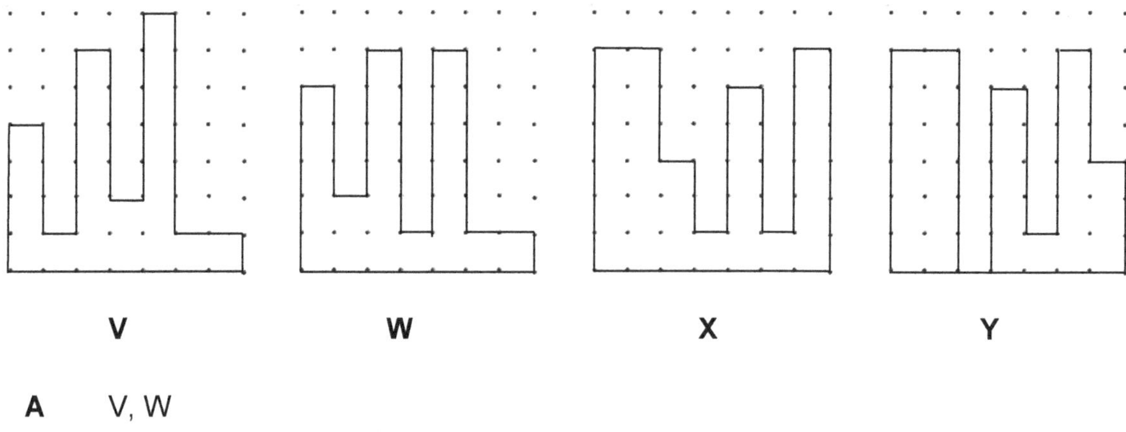

A V, W
B V, Y
C X, W
D X, V

27 All secondary school pupils should be required to take part in debating to involve disadvantaged communities in the democratic process.

Which one of the following, if true, most **weakens** the above argument?

A Debating helps build confidence and communication skills with others
B Joining debating can make children more aware of important social issues around the world
C Forcing students to participate may cause a great deal of stress and anxiety
D Debating can make students more familiar with political processes

28 Five children did a test with 5 difficult questions to answer.

- Kim was faster than Cherin but got 3 questions wrong
- Skye got all the questions right, but took the longest
- Jack finished second but got 2 questions wrong
- Cherin got one more question right than Jack but finished after him
- Natalie wasn't as fast as Jack but Jack was not as fast as Kim

If all the above statements are true, only one of the statements below can be true. Which one?

A Cherin got the fewest questions right
B Cherin got only one question wrong
C Kim was not the first to finish
D Kim got more questions right than Skye

29 Year 6 collected information on their grade's favourite sport.

Method	Number of Pupils
Tennis	33
Football	19
Swimming	?
Hockey	34
Running	55

The average is 37. How many students liked swimming the most?

A 35
B 38
C 44
D 28

30 The use of social media can connect many people together depending on their interests and hobbies hence making it a great place to make new friends and gain new perspectives.

Which one of the following, if true, most **weakens** the above argument?

A Social media makes spreading information a lot faster and more efficient
B Advertising on social media is an extra platform for smaller businesses
C Social media can create new and endless possibilities for young impressionable teenagers
D Social media leaves many teenagers vulnerable to cyberbullying

31 A motoring journalist was writing an article on car colours. He had the results of a survey, but the percentages did not add up to 100. However, the data were also shown as a pie chart with no labels.

Colour	Percent
Silver	50
White	20
Black	20
Red	10
Blue	5

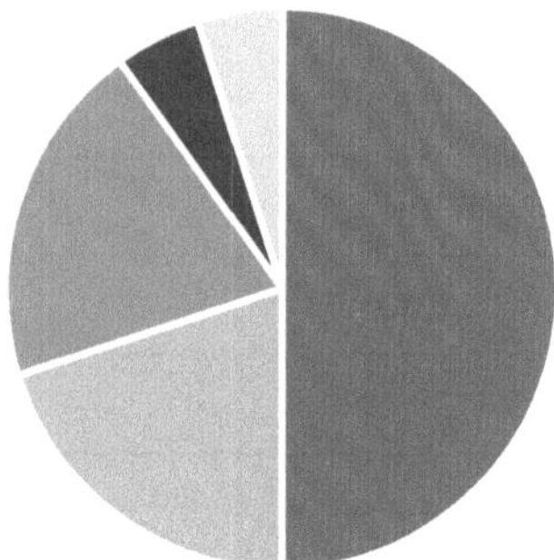

The pie chart is correct, but one of the values in the table is wrong. Which one?

A Silver
B White
C Black
D Red

32 Smartphones should not be allowed in schools as they will cause a distraction for both students and teachers. Even the classes might get disturbed if any student is found fiddling with their phone. The student will be at a loss as they will not be able to keep up with the class.

Which one of the following statements, if true, most **weakens** the above argument?

A Students might start browsing irrelevant, inappropriate websites and waste their time which can be utilised for studies
B Using smartphones can make education more accessible and keep parents in contact with their children
C Smartphones can be used for cheating during tests as many cases have been reported.
D Allowing smartphones in schools will give rise to unhealthy, unwanted competition as students with expensive and latest-model phones

33 Which shape was not used to make the following figure?

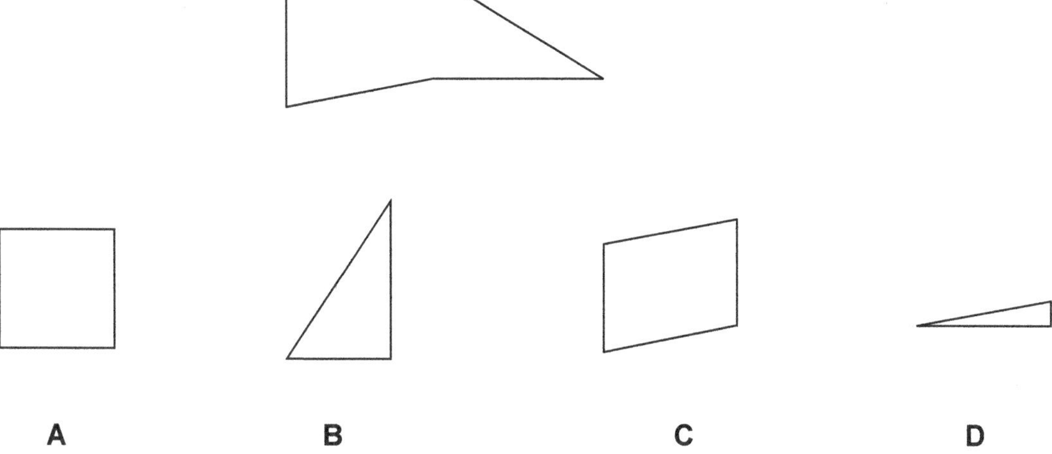

34 Divya wanted to see what hobbies were most popular at their school: skipping, rollerblading, ice skating or skateboarding. They did a survey of all the students and found the following:

- Everyone who liked rollerblading also liked ice skating
- Some people liked both ice skating and skipping
- No one liked both rollerblading and skipping
- There were more people who only liked ice skating than people who only liked skipping
- All skateboarders players also liked rollerblading

Which was the most popular hobby?

A Rollerblading
B Skipping
C Ice Skating
D Skateboarding

35 I am inside one of 3 houses. On the roof of each house, I have written 2 statements, some true, some false. However, no more than 1 statement on each roof is false.

House 1	House 2	House 3
My name is Lisa	I am not here	My name is Faith
I am not here	I am in house 3	I am not in house 1

Which one of the following statements must be true?

A My name is Lisa
B I am in house 1
C I am in house 3
D My name is Faith

36 China and Nepal jointly announced a new official height for Mount Everest on Tuesday, ending a disagreement between the two nations. The new height of the world's highest peak is 8848.86m, which is slightly more than Nepal's previous measurement and about 4m higher than China's.

What is the underlying assumption made by the above argument?

A The two countries are still having disagreements.
B Nepal and China overestimated the height of Mount Everest.
C China and Nepal previously could not agree on the height of Mount Everest.
D This was the only disagreement between these two countries.

37 A L plate driver recorded their driving process in a month.

Date	Odometer (km)		Time		
	Start	Finish	Start	Finish	Total (hrs)
21/06/21	11000	11060	10:00	11:00	1.0
28/06/21	12900	13000	9:30	11:30	2.0
05/07/21	15050	15200	17:30	19:00	1.5
12/07/21	16700	17000	13:00	17:00	4.0

On which day did the driver travel the most in 1 hour assuming that their speed was consistent?

A 21/06/21
B 28/06/21
C 05/07/21
D 12/07/21

38 Choose the next figure in this sequence.

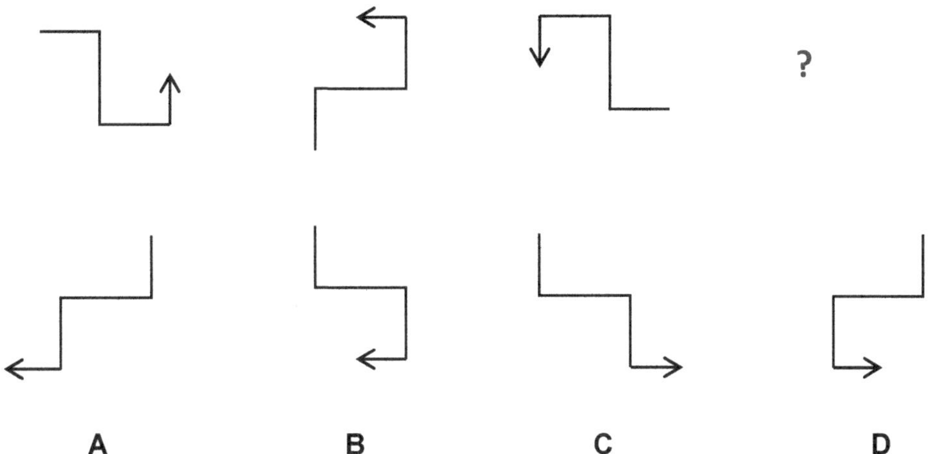

A **B** **C** **D**

39 Banning junk food in schools could encourage students to eat more healthy food. This could reduce the prevalence of mental health problems among students.

Which one of the following statements, if true, most **weakens** the above argument?

A Junk food increases the risk of diabetes, especially in younger children
B Some students may not have as much access to food due to the cost of healthier foods
C It would decrease the frequency of heart disease and other related diseases
D Eating junk food can negatively affect brain function in young children and hence their education

40 I want to send a parcel to my friend through Australia Post. The post office lists the rates to help me know how much it will cost to send a package, which is shown below:

Description	Rate
First 600 grams of a parcel	$3.80
Each additional 300 grams	$1.50
Standard postage fee	$3

If my parcel weighs 1.8 kilograms, and I am required to pay the standard postage fee, how much will it cost to send my parcel to my friend?

A $8.30
B $12.80
C $14.80
D $15.60

Selective Practice Test Paper
Thinking Skills 6 – Answer Sheet

Fill in the appropriate circle for your chosen answer

Eg.. A B C D
○ ● ○ ○

Use a pencil. If you make a mistake, erase thoroughly and try again.

NAME : **SCORE:**

1 A B C D ○○○○	11 A B C D ○○○○	21 A B C D ○○○○	31 A B C D ○○○○
2 A B C D ○○○○	12 A B C D ○○○○	22 A B C D ○○○○	32 A B C D ○○○○
3 A B C D ○○○○	13 A B C D ○○○○	23 A B C D ○○○○	33 A B C D ○○○○
4 A B C D ○○○○	14 A B C D ○○○○	24 A B C D ○○○○	34 A B C D ○○○○
5 A B C D ○○○○	15 A B C D ○○○○	25 A B C D ○○○○	35 A B C D ○○○○
6 A B C D ○○○○	16 A B C D ○○○○	26 A B C D ○○○○	36 A B C D ○○○○
7 A B C D ○○○○	17 A B C D ○○○○	27 A B C D ○○○○	37 A B C D ○○○○
8 A B C D ○○○○	18 A B C D ○○○○	28 A B C D ○○○○	38 A B C D ○○○○
9 A B C D ○○○○	19 A B C D ○○○○	29 A B C D ○○○○	39 A B C D ○○○○
10 A B C D ○○○○	20 A B C D ○○○○	30 A B C D ○○○○	40 A B C D ○○○○

BLANK PAGE

Selective Practice Test Paper
Thinking Skills 7 – Answer Sheet

Fill in the appropriate circle for your chosen answer

Eg.. A B C D
○ ● ○ ○

Use a pencil. If you make a mistake, erase thoroughly and try again.

NAME : **SCORE:**

1	A B C D ○○○○	11	A B C D ○○○○	21	A B C D ○○○○	31	A B C D ○○○○
2	A B C D ○○○○	12	A B C D ○○○○	22	A B C D ○○○○	32	A B C D ○○○○
3	A B C D ○○○○	13	A B C D ○○○○	23	A B C D ○○○○	33	A B C D ○○○○
4	A B C D ○○○○	14	A B C D ○○○○	24	A B C D ○○○○	34	A B C D ○○○○
5	A B C D ○○○○	15	A B C D ○○○○	25	A B C D ○○○○	35	A B C D ○○○○
6	A B C D ○○○○	16	A B C D ○○○○	26	A B C D ○○○○	36	A B C D ○○○○
7	A B C D ○○○○	17	A B C D ○○○○	27	A B C D ○○○○	37	A B C D ○○○○
8	A B C D ○○○○	18	A B C D ○○○○	28	A B C D ○○○○	38	A B C D ○○○○
9	A B C D ○○○○	19	A B C D ○○○○	29	A B C D ○○○○	39	A B C D ○○○○
10	A B C D ○○○○	20	A B C D ○○○○	30	A B C D ○○○○	40	A B C D ○○○○

BLANK PAGE

Selective Practice Test Paper
Thinking Skills 8 – Answer Sheet

Fill in the appropriate circle for your chosen answer

Eg.. A B C D
○ ● ○ ○

Use a pencil. If you make a mistake, erase thoroughly and try again.

NAME : **SCORE:**

1	A B C D ○○○○	11	A B C D ○○○○	21	A B C D ○○○○	31	A B C D ○○○○
2	A B C D ○○○○	12	A B C D ○○○○	22	A B C D ○○○○	32	A B C D ○○○○
3	A B C D ○○○○	13	A B C D ○○○○	23	A B C D ○○○○	33	A B C D ○○○○
4	A B C D ○○○○	14	A B C D ○○○○	24	A B C D ○○○○	34	A B C D ○○○○
5	A B C D ○○○○	15	A B C D ○○○○	25	A B C D ○○○○	35	A B C D ○○○○
6	A B C D ○○○○	16	A B C D ○○○○	26	A B C D ○○○○	36	A B C D ○○○○
7	A B C D ○○○○	17	A B C D ○○○○	27	A B C D ○○○○	37	A B C D ○○○○
8	A B C D ○○○○	18	A B C D ○○○○	28	A B C D ○○○○	38	A B C D ○○○○
9	A B C D ○○○○	19	A B C D ○○○○	29	A B C D ○○○○	39	A B C D ○○○○
10	A B C D ○○○○	20	A B C D ○○○○	30	A B C D ○○○○	40	A B C D ○○○○

BLANK PAGE

Selective Practice Test Paper
Thinking Skills 9 – Answer Sheet

Fill in the appropriate circle for your chosen answer

Eg.. A B C D
○ ● ○ ○

Use a pencil. If you make a mistake, erase thoroughly and try again.

NAME : **SCORE:**

1	A B C D ○○○○	11	A B C D ○○○○	21	A B C D ○○○○	31	A B C D ○○○○
2	A B C D ○○○○	12	A B C D ○○○○	22	A B C D ○○○○	32	A B C D ○○○○
3	A B C D ○○○○	13	A B C D ○○○○	23	A B C D ○○○○	33	A B C D ○○○○
4	A B C D ○○○○	14	A B C D ○○○○	24	A B C D ○○○○	34	A B C D ○○○○
5	A B C D ○○○○	15	A B C D ○○○○	25	A B C D ○○○○	35	A B C D ○○○○
6	A B C D ○○○○	16	A B C D ○○○○	26	A B C D ○○○○	36	A B C D ○○○○
7	A B C D ○○○○	17	A B C D ○○○○	27	A B C D ○○○○	37	A B C D ○○○○
8	A B C D ○○○○	18	A B C D ○○○○	28	A B C D ○○○○	38	A B C D ○○○○
9	A B C D ○○○○	19	A B C D ○○○○	29	A B C D ○○○○	39	A B C D ○○○○
10	A B C D ○○○○	20	A B C D ○○○○	30	A B C D ○○○○	40	A B C D ○○○○

BLANK PAGE

Selective Practice Test Paper
Thinking Skills 10 – Answer Sheet

Fill in the appropriate circle for your chosen answer

Eg.. A B C D
○ ● ○ ○

Use a pencil. If you make a mistake, erase thoroughly and try again.

NAME : **SCORE:**

1	A B C D ○ ○ ○ ○	11	A B C D ○ ○ ○ ○	21	A B C D ○ ○ ○ ○	31	A B C D ○ ○ ○ ○
2	A B C D ○ ○ ○ ○	12	A B C D ○ ○ ○ ○	22	A B C D ○ ○ ○ ○	32	A B C D ○ ○ ○ ○
3	A B C D ○ ○ ○ ○	13	A B C D ○ ○ ○ ○	23	A B C D ○ ○ ○ ○	33	A B C D ○ ○ ○ ○
4	A B C D ○ ○ ○ ○	14	A B C D ○ ○ ○ ○	24	A B C D ○ ○ ○ ○	34	A B C D ○ ○ ○ ○
5	A B C D ○ ○ ○ ○	15	A B C D ○ ○ ○ ○	25	A B C D ○ ○ ○ ○	35	A B C D ○ ○ ○ ○
6	A B C D ○ ○ ○ ○	16	A B C D ○ ○ ○ ○	26	A B C D ○ ○ ○ ○	36	A B C D ○ ○ ○ ○
7	A B C D ○ ○ ○ ○	17	A B C D ○ ○ ○ ○	27	A B C D ○ ○ ○ ○	37	A B C D ○ ○ ○ ○
8	A B C D ○ ○ ○ ○	18	A B C D ○ ○ ○ ○	28	A B C D ○ ○ ○ ○	38	A B C D ○ ○ ○ ○
9	A B C D ○ ○ ○ ○	19	A B C D ○ ○ ○ ○	29	A B C D ○ ○ ○ ○	39	A B C D ○ ○ ○ ○
10	A B C D ○ ○ ○ ○	20	A B C D ○ ○ ○ ○	30	A B C D ○ ○ ○ ○	40	A B C D ○ ○ ○ ○

BLANK PAGE

Selective Practice Test Answers
Thinking Skills 6

Question	Answer	Explanation
1	C	For these questions, it helps to trace the outline of different shapes onto the options. For this question Option C cannot be made, as the given shapes cannot form with 4x2 rectangle without overlapping.
2	B	The argument establishes that public speaking is a source of fear for many, however it provides many benefits and is important. Options A and D are incorrect as they weaken the argument. Option C seems to strengthen the argument, but it actually weakens it as it provides a counterpoint to the negative aspect. Option B is correct as it is the only option that supports the argument. It is important to remember for this question type; an option that agrees with the argument will strengthen it, and an argument that contradicts the argument will weaken it – it doesn't matter if the argument is positive or negative.
3	A	To find the annual cost of hot air systems, divide the total cost by the number of years. $\$15,000 \div 3 = \$5,000$ $\$10,000 \div 2 = \$5,000$ $\$25,000 \div 5 = \$5,000$
4	B	For this question type, the claim is correct if every Yes for the first question is matched by a Yes for the second question. As such, if there is a Yes in the first column we must know if there is a Yes in the second column, and if there is a No in the second column we must know if there is a Yes in the first column. Dye 1 has a Yes in the first column, so we must know a); and Dye 3 has a No in the second column, so we must know c).
5	A	If Nelly does not write notes, she is less well prepared for her class tests, meaning she should do worse. Doing badly on her class means she is less prepared for the final, and will likely score below 80%. Therefore, Option A is correct.
6	C	IF likes apple THEN doesn't like cranberry IF likes cranberry THEN likes guava IF likes orange THEN likes apple Option C is correct as it contradicts the third statement.

7	D	The argument establishes that if a playlist has less than 7 songs, it will play random songs that are not on the playlist. Both Diana and Cam think that a random song must have been added, so they are both wrong.
8	A	Each triangular quarter will have two holes near the edge, which only Option A possesses.
9	A	The argument says that most inkjet printers are sold at a low price. Options B and C are irrelevant. However, Option A proposes that owning a printer is not cheap due to the price of ink, thus weaking the argument. For this question, it is important to note that the argument is about the cost to buyers, while Option D is about the cost of production. Although the two are linked, Option A is better because it is about the cost to buyers.
10	B	Minghao handed his art in late, so would not be considered for the competition. This means that even if his artwork was the best, it wouldn't be judged and it would not be on the people's choice ballot. As such, Option B is the only reasonable explanation.
11	D	The oldest person among the group is 25. The second statement reveals that they are the third of three people to the right of the 19-year-old, so they must be in position 5.
12	C	The chart shows one party with half the vote, or 50 out of 100 people. The only town in which one party got 50 votes is Castle Hill.
13	C	
14	B	The statement establishes that only X's and O's are used in the program, so a W being on the board means that there is an error and neither party can win. As such, Naomi's statement is incorrect. Maddie points out this error in Naomi's reasoning, so is correct.
15	D	Although a class monitor is appointed each week, it is not stated that a student cannot be a class monitor twice. Option D reveals this mistake. Option C is factually correct, but does not address the mistake at all, so is not the correct answer.
16	D	

17	B	IF enjoys grapes THEN doesn't enjoy oranges (and vice versa) IF enjoys bananas THEN enjoys grapes IF enjoys oranges THEN enjoys apples More people enjoy bananas than apples The first three statements split students into two groups, bananas / grapes, and oranges / apples; and the fourth reveals that the first group is larger. However, bananas are a subset of grapes – everyone that enjoys bananas enjoys grapes, but not everyone that enjoys grapes enjoys bananas. As such, grapes must be the most popular.
18	A	The argument states that coding is a valuable skill for employees to have. Option A is the only one to address this, so is correct. The other three options are about how many people can learn to code, however the argument does not touch on this matter.
19	D	The logic process can be written as three statements: War -> peace, therefore freedom -> slavery, therefore ignorance -> strength It is important to note that the process flows from left to right, so each statement relies on previous ones being true. Additionally, only peace, freedom, and strength are affected by the process. That is, there will be freedom and ignorance regardless of whether war is peace or not. Given this, the process can be restated as: Peace leads to slavery leads to strength Option D is correct here, as it says that if there is no peace there can be no slavery. It is also possible to rule out the other options, as they do not follow the logic within the restated process.
20	D	Depth initially increases quickly, but slows down. As such, the container must be narrow at the bottom and progressively widen towards the top.
21	B	Taking away the votes that the members used for themselves, we find that Aiden has 3 votes, and Belinda and Chris have 1 each. As Dianne voted for Chris, Aiden must have voted for Belinda (he cannot use both votes on himself), and the other three voted for Aiden. Belinda's two votes are from herself and Aiden, so Chris cannot have voted for her.
22	B	

23	A	It can be concluded from this statement that anyone with at least 4 years' experience will be accepted before anyone that auditions is considered. As such, Option A presents the only valid reason for Joshua being able to join. Although Option B may appear right, it requires the assumption that the school has some way of judging the prior performance of experienced guitar players. It is important to remember that Selective exams will never require you to make extra assumptions, and that you should only work with the information provided in the question.
24	C	If we let x be the amount of rose water that Renuka gets, $0.5x + x + 2x = 1050$ $3.5x = 1050$ $x = 300$
25	D	The argument is that technology benefits today's society, helping us communicate, learn, and think. Option A is factually incorrect, and Options B and C strengthen the argument by providing positives of technology. Option D is correct, as it is the only one to suggest that technology has a negative impact.
26	A	To solve this question type, it helps to visualise the net as a folded cube and seeing which option fits. If not, you can use the process of elimination to determine whether the options are possible. Opposite faces on a cube will never be seen in the same picture, as they do not share an edge. To work out what is opposite a face, find the face that is two away from it. As such, Options B and C are wrong because 2 and 3 are opposites, and Option D is wrong because 1 and 6 are opposites. Option A then must be correct.
27	B	For two shapes to fit together, any feature in one shape must be matched by an opposite feature in the other shape. If part of one shape sticks out, the other shape must have a hole there. The features in 1 and 3 match up, so Option B must be correct.
28	B	The order of finishers and their deaths is as follows: Luddy (least) Ashi (3) Isabel (3) Guillaume (2nd least) Nick (5) Option B is correct.
29	D	There are 15 people eating, meaning the prices will be in the 13-20 category. As such, $5 \times \$10 + 10 \times \$15 = \$200$
30	A	

31	A	10th Century or prior: $480 \times \frac{1}{5} = 96$ 11th to 15th Century: $480 \times \frac{1}{8} = 60$ After the 19th Century: 210 16th to 19th Century: $480 - 96 - 60 - 210 = 114$
32	D	IF likes 44 homes THEN doesn't like hopscotch IF likes tag THEN likes hopscotch IF likes Marco Polo THEN likes 44 homes Option D is correct. It is not explicitly stated that all children like a sport, so it is possible for Vern to dislike both. However, the other three options all violate one of the statements, making Option D the most correct answer
33	C	
34	B	The argument says that dogs provide are not just companions, they also provide many emotional benefits to owners. Options A, C, and D all describe negative aspects of owning a dog, so weaken the argument. Option B is correct is it mentions the emotional benefit of reduced stress.
35	A	The statement suggests that each year possesses its own language, and that a given year's words are spoken in that language. Option A is correct, as the word spoken five years ago would be part of the language from five years ago.
36	B	Profit per ticket: $\$45 - \$27 - \$7 - \$4 = \$7$ Total profit: $120 \times \$7 = \$840$
37	A	In this passage, the author describes the calmness she feels around bees. However, this not being her usual reaction implies that bees usually scare her. As such, Option A is correct. Options B and D are irrelevant to the passage. Option C is described within the passage rather than being an assumption. It is important to remember that the correct answer for this type of question will not be described within the passage, it will instead be implied at some point.
38	B	
39	D	The passage says that the top 3 dancers are selected for each end of term performance, however it does not mention that dancers will not be selected if they have been in the top 3 previously. Option D is correct, as it points out this flaw in Anne's logic.
40	C	10% of Bondia's population is 400,000, and 20% of its area is 4,000 kilometres squared. The only island with a population less than 400,000 and an area of more than 4,000 is Dalton.

Selective Practice Test Answers
Thinking Skills 7

Question	Answer	Explanation
1	A	A starts off with an inclined section, which then gets steeper (i.e. the cyclist is moving faster) before it flattens out (i.e. the cyclist is taking a break for 10 minutes)
2	B	The argument states that piercings are recognised as unprofessional and therefore if people have multiple, they should take some down. Option A provides an assumption which doesn't strengthen nor weaken the argument. Option C strengthens the argument while Option D is an incorrect statement. Option B is correct because it states piercings are a way of expressing themselves and therefore weakens the argument in suggesting they should not take them down.
3	D	Option D is the most correct option. This is as, Politician Jane does not address the issue Politician Albert has raised and instead chooses to discuss his own lifestyle.
4	B	
5	A	The information in the box suggests if the device can detect internet reception based on if it shows signal or not. Kate draws the correct reasoning by establishing the device is unable to detect internet reception since the device did not show a signal. Ashley's reasoning was incorrect as she draws the conclusion that the area did not have any internet reception instead of the device's ability to detect internet.
6	B	Option B: - Medicine taken in October = 3.0mL - Medicine taken in January = 4.0mL Difference in medicine taken: 4.0mL – 3.0mL = 1.0mL
7	D	Option D is the correct option. The statement describes Alfred Nobel's great achievements through his inventions and his creation of prizes. This therefore provides Nobel's name with a positive connotation.
8	C	The argument states that drinking bottled spring water led to improved performance over regular tap water, therefore concluding the benefits of buying spring water. Option A, B and D strengthens the argument. Option C is correct as by drawing similarities of the two types of water, it weakens the argument.

9	D	The argument above states it would benefit technology companies to make their devices more suitable for the older generation.
10	A	A pattern under the rules must be recognised. Right arrow is drawn to rotate 'shape A' 90 degrees clockwise. Plus Shape is drawn to make 'shape A' smaller. Left arrow is draw to flip 'shape A' vertically White right arrow is drawn to make 'shape A' larger. In Row 3, we want to make 'shape A' bigger, and therefore the missing rule must be the White right arrow. Therefore, Option A is correct.
11	A	If a word is the same in Sanshi and Shelo, it must also be the same in Sanskari. Therefore, Patrick's word must be common to all three and therefore cannot be a greeting. As such, he is correct. However, if a word is the same in Sanshi and Sanskari, it does not have to be the same in Shelo. As such, this word may be a greeting, and Katy is incorrect.
12	B	It is established that everyone who likes volleyball also liked cricket, this suggests volleyball is a subset of cricket and there were students who liked cricket who didn't like volleyball. Therefore, Option A and D is incorrect. Since there were more people who only liked cricket than those who only liked soccer, cricket was a more popular sport than soccer. From this, Option C is incorrect. Therefore, Option B is correct.
13	C	Height wise – you can fit two layers into the parallelogram Length wise – you can fit 15 tiles Total = 15 x 2 = 30
14	B	Area of black triangle in one tile: $36cm^2$ / 4 = $9cm^2$ The total area of the black triangles would therefore be: 30 x $9cm^2$ = $270cm^2$
15	B	Option A is incorrect as not all make-believe worlds *must* have their own rules. Option C is incorrect as the world does not *have* to be bizarre for it to be entertaining. Option D provides an assumption which does not conclude any fact about the passage's statements on rules. Option B correctly summarises the passages opinion on rules for fictional worlds.
16	C	Option C is correct as it determines Sarah's mistake in determining that the statistics is a representation of the effectiveness of these antitheft devices.

17	D	The argument establishes a similarity which groups ducks and chickens into the same category, however, then differentiates the two types of birds through their ability to quack. This is paralleled in Option D where the similarity between water and soft drinks being liquids are categorised together. Where the flavour between the two differentiates the two liquids.
18	D	Alayna's reasoning is incorrect as the academical comparison between her friend other women in her first year of university is not relevant to the information in the box in comparing high schools. Lizzie's reasoning is incorrect because if her friend achieved a higher score than her friends in other schools then she should have gone to a girl's high school. Therefore, neither Alayna nor Lizzie have correct reasonings.
19	D	
20	C	The argument states that increasing the number of armed police officers is also increasing the rate of this certain crime. Option A and B state the experience and skill level of police officers but do not strengthen nor weaken the argument. Option D is a statement but does not contribute to the argument. Option C is correct as it directly contradicts the argument provided by the passage.
21	A	Option A is the most correct option. The scientist has made a mistake in drawing the conclusion that food irradiation is 'definitely' safe from not having evidence that it is unsafe. Evidence must be provided that food irradiation is safe to have a definitive conclusion on the safety of food irradiation.
22	C	KVB -> Linfield (\$3) then Linfield -> North beach (\$6) \$3 + \$6 = \$9
23	D	The argument states that large brains are a representation of the animal's intelligence, it expresses the Beluga Whale has a higher intelligence than humans. From this, Option A, B and C all strengthen the argument and is therefore incorrect. Option D weakens the argument by suggesting intelligence is not the reason to large brains.
24	C	Statement 1 is true. Since some dinosaurs were warm-blooded and reptiles are cold-blooded. Therefore, not all dinosaurs may have been warm-blooded. Statement 2 is true. Since discovering some dinosaurs were warm-blooded, therefore some reptiles may be warm-blooded. Therefore, both statements are correct.

25	A	First Year = 1000 Second Year = 80% of 1000 + 10 = 810 Third Year = 80% of 810 + 10 = 658
26	A	The argument states criminals tend to take left turns to lose police car chases. Option B and C are statements which weaken the argument and is therefore incorrect. Option D contradicts the given argument and is therefore incorrect. Option A strengthens the argument by providing an explanation to why criminals choose not to turn right. Therefore, Option A is correct.
27	D	
28	D	Option D is correct. The day begins as a high temperature and remains that temperature as time goes on. A steep incline is seen due to the drop in temperature from the storm. Then an increase in temperature is seen by another ascending incline.
29	B	Option B is correct. The passage establishes how proper equipment is expensive especially if the house has older equipment. The passage recommends to lower taxes in households, this suggesting the main reason that the appropriate equipment is not bought due to financial difficulties.
30	C	8415 + 8491+ 9950 + 27983 = 54839
31	C	The argument states that food security is experienced all around the world. Options A does not contribute to the argument and is therefore incorrect. Options B and D provides a comment towards food security and does not strengthen nor weaken the argument provided. Option C strengthens the argument and is therefore the correct answer.
32	D	The argument states zoos are unsuitable places for animals to live in and zoos should be closed. Options B and C strengthen the argument. Option A although provides a reason to why zoos should remain open, it does not provide a reasonable argument to weaken the argument. Option D is the most correct, this is as it comments on a counterargument on how zoos provide endangered species a safe location and therefore most weakens the argument.
33	B	
34	B	Pattern: 3, 7, 11 (+4) Rule: $N^{th} \rightarrow 3 + 4 \times (N - 1)$ Let N = 6 to find the 6th shape: 3 + 4 x 5 = 23
35	B	The argument states that speed-reading techniques are effective however provides limited benefits to many readers who want to gain an understanding of what they read. Options A and C strengthens the argument.

<table>
<tr><td>36</td><td>D</td><td>Option A is incorrect as Tribe Z is not pure vegetarians.
Option B is an assumption which cannot be guaranteed true and therefore incorrect.
Option C is an assumption which cannot be guaranteed true and therefore incorrect.
Therefore, none of the above is true.</td></tr>
<tr><td>37</td><td>C</td><td>Solid P: 8 blocks = 20secs

Using the unitary method:
- 2 blocks = 5 seconds

Since, Solid S has 18 blocks
9 x 5sec = 45 seconds</td></tr>
<tr><td>38</td><td>A</td><td>The passage concludes that darts differ greatly to other Olympic sports due to their more relaxing nature in comparison to the competitive nature of Olympic sports.

Option A is the best statement to conclude the passage.</td></tr>
<tr><td>39</td><td>A</td><td>The argument states scientists are unable to explain the fastest serve in tennis and the reaction time of the server. Options B and C weaken the argument. Option D is a statement which does not contribute to the argument. Option A is the most correct as it explains science's inability to explain every expectation provided towards humans.</td></tr>
<tr><td>40</td><td>D</td><td>At the beginning of Year 1, there were 1000 people.

<table>
<tr><td rowspan="2"></td><td colspan="7">Year</td></tr>
<tr><td>Year 1</td><td>Year 2</td><td>Year 3</td><td>Year 4</td><td>Year 5</td><td>Year 6</td><td>Year 7</td></tr>
<tr><td>Change in population</td><td>-70</td><td>-50</td><td>-30</td><td>-10</td><td>+10</td><td>+30</td><td>+50</td></tr>
<tr><td>Overall population</td><td>930</td><td>870</td><td>850</td><td>840</td><td>850</td><td>870</td><td>930</td></tr>
</table>

By calculating the change in population, the overall population can be determined.

Therefore, Option D can be identified as the correct graph.</td></tr>
</table>

Selective Practice Test Answers
Thinking Skills 8

Question	Answer	Explanation
1	A	The passage argues that social networking sites are good for maintaining existing connections and making new ones. Option A reinforces this idea, thus strengthens the argument.
2	B	It is stated that whenever Leslie goes to the diner she will go to the markets. However, it is not mentioned that every trip to the markets is preceded by a visit to the diner. As such, Tom is incorrect but Andy is correct.
3	B	$3 + 2 + 5 + 10 = 20$, so one entry in the Bicycle column is incorrect. $20 + 10 + 3 + 30 = 63$, so the value of 3 must be incorrect.
4	D	Only Asus and Samsung meet the memory requirement of 6GB. Of those, only Samsung has a 15 inch screen.
5	A	
6	A	The argument states that malaria can develop for up to 120 days after exposure to the parasite. However if the parasite could travel to other cells that live for longer, a fever that appears after 120 days may in fact be caused my malaria. Hence, Option A is correct.
7	A	The government is conducting a large spending project to prepare for future growth, however Hector is critical of it due to its lack of immediate success. Option A is correct as it points out that these projects are likely to be effective in the longer-term, rather than immediately.
8	D	From the first picture to the second, the cube is flipped upside down. As such, the white square must be opposite the black one.
9	A	The triangle must be pointing towards the white circle and away from the cross. Additionally, the triangle must be pointing down when it is on the left of the black square.
10	A	The argument suggests that we should focus on stopping wars rather than paying refugees to live in Europe due to the pressure it places on public services. Options B, C, and D all serve to weaken the argument, so are incorrect. Option A is correct, as it highlights that refugees may face danger in their new countries too.

11	A	If Andy misses the bus, he cannot get to school and will not receive the award at assembly. Option A is impossible.
12	B	The folded segment has been horizontally mirrored. As such, the left section of the unfolded shape will look like the folded section. Option B must be correct.
13	A	A: N/A B: Front view C: Side view D: Top view
14	C	IF likes Twisties THEN likes Cheezels IF likes Cheezels THEN likes Chips Likes Cheezels OR likes Crackers If Lassie likes Twisties, she will also like Cheezels and therefore will not like Crackers. It is important to remember that the logic in these questions only works in one direction – all that like Twisties like Cheezels, but not all that like Cheezels will like Twisties.
15	A	**Alex: Year 1 – 100%, Year 2 – 150%** Benny: Year 1 – 100%, Year 2 – 25% Caden: Year 1 – 300%, Year 2 – 25% Dorothy: Year 1 – 33.3%, Year 2 – 25% This question can be done visually, but the exact values were calculated using the formula: $Change(\%) = (Year\ 2\ -\ Year\ 1)/(Year\ 1)$
16	D	The argument states that although painkillers are effective at reducing flu symptomps, they may prolong the sickness and increase transmission to others. Option D provides a reason for transmission to occur, therefore best strengthens the argument.
17	B	Jessica must catch the 15:02 bus from Burwood to arrive before 16:00, so has to arrive at Burwood at 14:22 to spend 40 minutes shopping. As such, she must catch the 13:17 bus from Ashfield.
18	C	Becky won the championship, but cannot qualify or be included in the wild card as she did not compete in nationals. Her statement is incorrect. Jacob didn't win nationals and wasn't champion, however he may still be selected as the wild card entry. His statement is also incorrect.
19	D	To have Friday afternoon free, Zoe must do Colouring in the morning. This means that she has to participate in Swimming on Tuesday afternoon, Athletics on Monday afternoon, and Hiking on Wednesday afternoon. This leaves Painting for Thursday afternoon.

20	B	The argument attaches a sense of success to possessions. This carries the assumption that success will result in wealth, which can then be used to buy possessions. In this sense, a large number of possessions is a signal for success, as only those with a lot of success and therefore wealth can buy many possessions.
21	B	Mr Lee has not controlled enough variables in his experiment. In other words, he has not ensured that the amount of study and practice is consistent among the groups, and this mistake is pointed out in Option B.
22	A	Coding and hardware skills are required to build a working laptop. Neither Sam nor Sally possess both skills, so neither will be able to build a working laptop. As such, both statements are incorrect.
23	B	Using the first four clues, the order of houses from left to right is: Danny: ?, Blue Andrew: PlayStation, ? ?: PC, Green Carly: ?, ? Ellie: ?, Brown It is then stated that Bruce likes to play the PC, so he must be in the middle.
24	A	The passage says that primary sources are those that are firsthand, recorded by a participant or observer, which implies that they are more reliable than secondary sources. Option A supports this notion by directly stating that they are the most reliable.
25	C	Musicians argue that Spotify is underpaying them for financial gain. Option C is the only one to weaken the argument, as it states that paying artists more would come at the expense of Spotify's profit.
26	C	Getting a different position in each race would mean a competitor earns a different number of points for each race. The points earned by each competitor in each race is as follows: Alice: 5, 1, 1, 2 Belinda: 1, 2, 2, 5 **Charlie: 2, 5, 3, 1** Daniel: 3, 3, 5, 3
27	C	The argument states that worldwide demand for ivory tusks has fallen; however it does not mention anything about supply, which is what is actually related to poaching. Option C correctly points out that although demand may fluctuate, supply will remain relatively constant, so poaching likely hasn't decreased.
28	D	Jessica has 10m of each colour. She needs 8m of red (3 dancers with 2m of red and 2 dancers with 1m of red), so will have 2m left over.

29	C	The ending balance of Vivian's bank account per month is as follows: Jan: $100 Feb: $0 **Mar: $300** Apr: $100 **May: $300** **Jun: $400**
30	B	IF dislikes PE THEN dislikes Science Maths > English Science < PE English > PE Combining these gives Maths > English > PE > Science, meaning Maths is the most popular.
31	A	If Erika's stream isn't clear, then it must be at a lower resolution than the 720p setting that would provide a clear picture. As such, Jiji is correct. If Erika's stream is on 480p then it is not fine, so she is incorrect.
32	D	All of the options associate a smell with particular sensations. Option D is incorrect as the feeling of rain is associated with cold, not warmth.
33	A	The argument concludes that the teaching of foreign languages in English schools is worse than other countries, as students who have never travelled outside of their countries have worse foreign language skills than their counterparts. However, poor performance may be due to other factors such as language spoken with friends or at home, which is pointed out in Option A.
34	A	If Pete and Melissa got the same overall scores, any difference in one game must be matched by an equal and opposite difference in the other. Pete is therefore correct, and Melissa is incorrect.
35	B	1-10: 5 11-20: 10 21-30: 20 31-40: 50 41-50: 20 51-60: 10 61-70: 0 71-80: 5 120 students own some amount of books, so 5 students must not own any.
36	C	The amount of the minutes the train spends stationary is $6 \times 3 + 4 \times 6 = 42$. It left Blacktown at 10:50am and arrived Central at 12:08pm, so spent 1 hour and 18 minutes to complete its journey. $78 - 42 = 36$, which is the number of minutes the train spent travelling.

37	D	The argument is that the government should prevent increases in house prices, as high house prices prevents many from owning a house and leaves those that do with large debts. Option D reinforces this issue by stating that house prices are becoming increasingly more unaffordable, so is correct.
38	A	The argument states that better teaching at private schools results in better exam performance, and thus higher acceptance rates into top universities.
39	C	The passage states that people staying inside due to the virus has resulted in fewer people shopping in person, meaning physical stores are unable to pay for rent. This carries the assumption that stores do not have online counterparts so physical shopping isn't being replaced by online shopping, which is seen in Option C.
40	A	The statement is that an apology will help the community grow, however it was long overdue. This allows us to draw the conclusion that the apology should have been made a long time ago.

Selective Practice Test Answers
Thinking Skills 9

<table>
<tr><th>Question</th><th>Answer</th><th>Explanation</th></tr>
<tr><td>1</td><td>D</td><td>The total number of books = 280
The average number of books per hour = 280/8 = 35</td></tr>
<tr><td>2</td><td>D</td><td>The argument suggests that people in America are made up of unhealthy food and an increased number of education programs would lead to healthier diets. Option D is therefore a correct assumption to the argument.</td></tr>
<tr><td>3</td><td>D</td><td>The argument states that due to a fall in demand for turtle shell jewellery, there would be a decline in turtle poaching. Option A does not directly weaken nor strengthen the argument and therefore is incorrect. Both Option B and Option C strengthens the argument. Option D is correct as it offers reasons to why turtle poaching would not decline and therefore weakening the argument.</td></tr>
<tr><td>4</td><td>A</td><td>The order of the images was changed from: 1 2 3 -> 3 1 2
Image 2 was rotated 180 degrees clockwise.
Image 3 was rotated 90 degrees clockwise.</td></tr>
<tr><td>5</td><td>C</td><td>Option C is incorrect as Meg collected more coins than Rebecca.</td></tr>
<tr><td>6</td><td>A</td><td>
<table>
<tr><th rowspan="2"></th><th colspan="5">Points</th></tr>
<tr><th>High Jump</th><th>100m</th><th>1500m</th><th>Long Jump</th><th>Total Points</th></tr>
<tr><td>Adam</td><td>2</td><td>4</td><td>5</td><td>2</td><td>13</td></tr>
<tr><td>Belinda</td><td>3</td><td>2</td><td>3</td><td>5</td><td>13</td></tr>
<tr><td>Chris</td><td>5</td><td>5</td><td>2</td><td>4</td><td>16</td></tr>
<tr><td>Dianne</td><td>2</td><td>2</td><td>2</td><td>2</td><td>8</td></tr>
</table>
Chris has the highest number of points and therefore wins.</td></tr>
<tr><td>7</td><td>C</td><td>The heart will not be visible on the cross section, and the rectangular prism on top is narrower than the cylinder so will be smaller. This is seen in Option C</td></tr>
<tr><td>8</td><td>D</td><td>The Principal assumes that school sports are detrimental to studying. Option D is the most correct answer as his argument does not recognise the benefits of sports and only focuses on the detrimental.</td></tr>
</table>

9	B	IF likes pink THEN likes purple IF likes blue THEN likes yellow IF likes yellow THEN dislikes orange IF likes purple THEN likes blue If Tessa likes purple then she will also like blue and yellow, therefore she will dislike orange. It is important to remember that the logic in these questions only works in one direction – all that like pink like purple, but not all that like purple will like pink.
10	A	Rule: Rotate shape 90 degrees anticlockwise.
11	A	The information in the box states: The sinking machine must operate for the pressing machine to start or else it would not be possible for the pressing machine to start. Therefore, only reasoning 1 is correct.
12	B	
13	A	To determine the shape reflected to the left, the shape is rotated 90 degrees anticlockwise.
14	B	The argument parallels two types of items in the same category in the first sentence (pork and chicken breasts). In the next sentence, some of that category is one of the types of items. ("Some meats are pork") The third sentence establishes that some of that category is, therefore, not the other type of item. ("Some meats are not chicken breasts") This parallels with Option B.
15	C	<table><tr><td>BEEN</td><td>FIND</td><td>MAKE</td><td>DOWN</td></tr><tr><td>2554</td><td>6944</td><td>3115</td><td>4534</td></tr></table> Option C is the word he is unsure about as 3115 could be CAKE or MAKE.
16	C	The lowest common multiple of 3 and 4 is 12. Therefore, Vince and Victor will see each other on the 12th day after Sunday. This means they will see each other at training on Thursday.
17	B	Posie's reasoning is incorrect as the information states the punishment will be decreased, not completed waived. Rosie's reasoning is correct as she is identifying a flaw in the system by stating motivations can be subjective and criminals may take advantage of this to get a decreased sentence.
18	D	Better safe than sorry refers to a principle of being wiser in being extra careful rather than regret it after if future problems occur.

19	D	A rectangular prism is a three-dimensional solid where all sides are rectangles. The original rectangular prism must have had the dimensions of: 8 x 7 x 4 = 224 blocks The current 3D shape has a total of 20 x 7 = 140 blocks (Face x breadth) 224 – 140 = 84 blocks. Therefore, Option D is correct.
20	A	In order of intelligence: Science Fiction Romance Fiction Action
21	C	The statement says that specialist farms only exist in dense cities, but it does not mention that dense cities must have had specialist farms. Option C is correct, as it points out this mistake.
22	D	From the first picture to the second, the cube is rotated to the right. As such, the circle must be opposite the triangle.
23	A	The argument states that sitting in rows in a classroom would help children to concentrate better as they see the teacher. Options B, C and D all strengthen the argument. While Option A weaken the argument by stating the formation of rows would still lead to children being distracted.
24	B	A square with 9 congruent squares would mean it would be 3 squares by 3 squares. Since the area of this square would be 225cm^2, each side would be 15cm x 15cm. This means the side of each square would be 5cm. The perimeter of the shape would be: 14 x 5cm = 70cm
25	B	100 cm / 5 = 20 sides. Option B has 20 sides.
26	B	The argument states that there are little steps to ensure success. Option B describes the large goal to success would be working up to this goal. Therefore, is the most correct answer.
27	C	The argument states that there are much less victims to violent crimes than the population would believe, and these fears are increased through television shows. Options A and D provide statistics to the crime but do not comment on the argument on television shows. Option B provides an assumption that these crimes are not researched, however this does not contribute to the argument. Option C is correct as it establishes the effect of TV shows by inducing unnecessary fear.

<table>
<tr><td>28</td><td>D</td><td>
<table>
<tr><th rowspan="2"></th><th colspan="5">Customer Number</th></tr>
<tr><th>1</th><th>2</th><th>3</th><th>4</th><th>5</th></tr>
<tr><td>Time delayed</td><td>15min</td><td>23min</td><td>15min</td><td>5min</td><td>25min</td></tr>
<tr><td>Compensation</td><td>$3</td><td>$5</td><td>$3</td><td>$0</td><td>$5</td></tr>
</table>

Total Compensation = 3 + 5 + 3 + 5 = $16</td></tr>
<tr><td>29</td><td>D</td><td>The information provided suggests that people with high blood pressure are more nervous and anxious. Jane assumes that due to his brother's 'hypertensive' personality; these traits make him have high blood pressure. Option D accurately describes Jane's mistake as despite high blood pressure causing these traits, not the other way around.</td></tr>
<tr><td>30</td><td>A</td><td>Plots 2, 5, and 7 are square; so the correct answer will have three square plots. This is seen in Option A.</td></tr>
<tr><td>31</td><td>B</td><td>Bob states he has "searched nearly the entire forest", meaning he has not covered all parts of the forest. However, the probability of trees may not necessarily be equal in all parts of the forest. It could be possible that Bob and Kaitlin searched a location where Maple Trees were more populous than Oak Trees. Therefore, Kaitlin has made a mistake in assuming more Oak Trees are required if there is a possibility that they have not found all the Oak Trees.</td></tr>
<tr><td>32</td><td>C</td><td>Discrimination occurs in the order of what is necessary, then what is not necessary or destructive, then what is destructive. In other words, discrimination of one must be preceded by the discrimination of the ones before this. Additionally, discrimination must occur for happiness to exist.
Using this, Options A, B, and D can all be eliminated as they violate the logic presented. As such, Option C must be correct, as it is impossible to only discriminate one thing.</td></tr>
<tr><td>33</td><td>B</td><td>The correct option will have slight variation in the height of the columns, and the last section will be the tallest. This is seen in Option B.</td></tr>
<tr><td>34</td><td>C</td><td>Boom quality > GE Electrics quality
Mango quality > Boom quality
GE Electrics price > Watt price
Boom price > Watt price
Mango price > Boom price
Maverick wants a relatively cheap monitor that is still good quality, so he will go for Boom.</td></tr>
</table>

35	D	IF likes dolls THEN likes teddy bears IF likes teddy bears THEN likes action figures IF likes action figures THEN like toy cars If ben likes teddy bears, then he will also like action figures and therefore toy cars. It is important to remember that the logic in these questions only works in one direction – all that like dolls like teddy bears, but not all that like teddy bears will like toy cars.
36	C	
37	B	Option A: $3 \times 3 \times 7 = 63$ **Option B:** $\boldsymbol{\pi \times 2^2 \times 7 = 87.96}$ Option C: $6 \times 4 \times 3 = 72$ Option D: $\pi \times 3^2 \times 2 = 56.55$
38	A	**Dennis:** $\mathbf{3 + 3 + 6 + 9 = 21}$ Andrew: $9 + 2 + 0 + 9 = 20$ Vivian: $1 + 4 + 7 + 8 = 20$ Jessica: $5 + 5 + 3 + 7 = 20$ It is important to remember that a working week is 5 days, so 20 working days is 4 weeks
39	A	Hip-Hop > R&B R&B > Blues Pop > Hip-Hop As such, Blues was the least popular.
40	B	Peter needs to copy 120 pages, and will be paying in the 50-149 range has he is printing 60 copies. As such, he must pay $2.40.

Selective Practice Test Answers
Thinking Skills 10

Question	Answer	Explanation
1	D	B and C are immediately eliminated as their middle section should be a diagonal shape rather than a square. A cannot be due to three shaded areas on the left side corner rather than just two which leaves D as the answer.
2	B	BCE = 2x3x5, YB = 25x2 therefore HR = 144
3	A	There are 12 shaded areas altogether, this immediately eliminates C as doubling it only produces 8 blocks. Both B and D do not produce the shaded area no matter how you position them.
4	A	C is not relevant. B and D weaken the argument.
5	D	The rule is to state dislike for the healthy option and present an alternative or issue with being healthy. A and B do not do so. C is not supporting the argument. D is the only one which provides a reason why Billy does not like exercising.
6	C	Jeans = 35 Skirts = 18 Jackets = 35 T-Shirts = 112 To solve for Jackets 70 – Jeans To solve for T-shirts 120 – Jeans – Jackets - Skirts
7	D	A cannot be as there is no discussion about his parents. C cannot be as he doesn't talk about the idea of learning from mistakes. B could be but it is a general statement so D has to be it as it specifically references Bob.
8	C	A, B and D all perceive beauty pageants in a negative light thus supporting the argument. C is the only one which sees the positive outcomes of participating thus is weaking the statement in question.
9	C	Logically the number of times others have not been caught does not impact Linda's ability to be caught as there are still ticket inspectors who will check.
10	C	A is possible with 3x2 1 and 1.5 B is possible with 3x2 1.5x2 D is possible with 3x3 and 1

11	B	Harry is correct as Milsons Point has only become accessible the past two weeks whilst he had gone to the drone show three weeks before. Chloe is correct as the harbour is one of the two places where the drone show can be seen.
12	A	Left to right Jimmy – Corrina – Teddy – Niall – Louis Numbering the dot points 1 – 4 the rules should be followed in this order: 1,2, 4 and 3 to get the layout
13	A	The argument's structure is: X has Y. Z is X. Therefore Z is Y. A is the best outcome as it links leaves to trees before introducing how plants also have leaves. Then makes the conclusion that plants can be trees. B, C and D do not follow the structure.
14	B	You will need to buy 5 jars to hit 1kg at either store. Coles basically does is buy 5 jars for the price of 4 which is $20. Woolworths is $25 at full price subtracted by 40% which is $10 being $15. 20-15 = $5 difference between the two stores.
15	B	A, C and D are all negative towards the argument, weakening it and leaving B as the only positive and strengthening option.
16	A	N T 14 m 10 m You are looking from the perspective of T looking to I
17	A	For someone who was in the Top 5 of the previous Athletics Carnival, they needed to do well in their first semester grades thus it means Paul must have done badly being A as he was second in the last Athletics Carnival. All other options are irrelevant.
18	D	The argument ends with highlighting how humans are the greatest cause of human life over any other species that can cause humans harm, yet sharks have been always seen as dangerous. This makes D the best conclusion as the shark's ability to harm humans should not be strongly demonised as it has been.
19	C	A is a side view, B is a front view and D is a bird's eye. C is an attempted bird's eye but is a block short.
20	A	((1x3)+(2x1)+(3x9)+(4x5)+(5x2)) / 20 = 3.1
21	D	Just add up 67000 + 84250 + 64500 = 215750 which is D

22	B	Use the DST (Distance, Speed, Time) pyramid We know the first part: D = 63km and S= 70km/h We are missing time and based on the triangle to find the time it is D/S 63/70 = 0.9 Remember time is in hours so 60 is used as there are 60 minutes in an hour 0.9 into fraction form is 90/100 or simplify to 9/10 $\frac{9}{10}$ x 60 = 54 mins Answer is B
23	C	B and D support the argument. A is not the strongest protection. C is the answer as it introduces an important aspect to jobs which are customers and needing to account for their views.
24	B	Guess and check using the equation of 2 x the number of birds + 4 x the number of sheep = 36
25	D	Lollies → Chocolate → Sour Candy (does not like Licorice) A, B and C do not follow the rules above, you cannot assume any dislikes other than licorice.
26	B	Looking at the shapes V can only work with Y as it has the longest piece which eliminates any other V and shapes combination, eliminating options A and D. Next looking at C, it cannot be due to the need for two towers of W to be next to each other, with one being one block shorter than the other which is not present in W eliminating C as an option. This leaves B.
27	C	A, C and D are all positive statements about debating, thus strengthening the argument leaving C as the only one which weakens the argument through its negative perception.
28	B	Speed from fastest to slowest based on statements: Kim → Jack → Cherin → Natalie → Skye Reading the statements, A is eliminated as Cherin had more questions correct than Jack. C cannot be based on the speed statements made. D cannot be as Skye got all questions correct. This leaves B.
29	C	If the mean of the 5 sports is 37, then the total number of students will be 5 x 37 = 185. Adding up the other numbers, you will find that it equals 141. 185-141= 44
30	D	A, B and C are positive statements whilst D is the only negative one, thus weakening the argument.

31	D	A is correct as it is half of the chart. White and Black are the same measurements which can be assumed as the two largest sectors after Silver. Red which is D is incorrect as there are two same sized small pieces and Blue is not an option so it can be assumed Red is the wrong value.
32	B	A, C and D are positively supporting the argument leaving B as the only option which negatively supports the argument, weakening it.
33	A	It cannot be A as it has no edges to form the small triangle seen at the bottom of the square section of the shape. B, c and D are all feasible in making the shape.
34	C	A and B are eliminated as no one liked both sports together, reducing popularity. It cannot be D as there is not enough information about who else could like the sport. Ice skating which is C is the answer as the number of people who only did ice skating is greater than only skipping.
35	C	C is the only option as all other options will not be true after the initial testing of one false statement under each house.
36	C	The underlying assumption is that both countries disagreed over the height of Mount Everest making C the answer closest to the assumption as it mentions both a disagreement and specifically cites Mount Everest.
37	C	Using the DST pyramid the missing value is speed. Subtract the start and end odometer times and then find each speed by doing distance / time. A = 60 km/h B = 50 km/h C = 100 km/h D = 75 km/h
38	D	A and B are eliminated as the arrow must point to the right. C does not have the line for a U shape with the arrow in the way D does eliminate C.
39	B	A, C and D all positively agree with the statement, strengthening it and leaving B as the only negative statement which weakens it.
40	B	Convert kg to g making the parcel 1800g. 1800 – 600 = 1200 1200/300 = 4 \$3+\$3.8+(4x1.5) = \$12.8